The Belt and Road Initiative
in the
Global Context

Series on China's Belt and Road Initiative

Print ISSN: 2591-7730
Online ISSN: 2591-7749

Series Editors: ZHENG Yongnian *(National University of Singapore, Singapore)*
Kerry BROWN *(King's College London, UK)*
WANG Yiwei *(Renmin University of China, China)*
LIU Weidong *(Chinese Academy of Sciences, China)*

This book series showcases the most up-to-date and significant research on China's Belt and Road Initiative (BRI) by leading scholars from inside and outside China. It presents a panoramic view on the BRI, from the perspectives of China's domestic policy, China's foreign investment, international relations, cultural cooperation and historical inheritance. As the first English book series on the BRI, this series offers a valuable English-language resource for researchers, policymakers, professionals and students to better understand the challenges and opportunities brought by the BRI.

Published:

Vol. 6   *The Belt and Road Initiative in the Global Context*
edited by WANG Linggui and ZHAO Jianglin

Vol. 5   *China's Belt and Road Initiative and Building the Community of Common Destiny*
edited by WANG Linggui and ZHAO Jianglin

Vol. 4   *Belt and Road Initiative: Chinese Version of "Marshall Plan"?*
by FENG Da Hsuan and LIANG Hai Ming

Vol. 3   *Silk Road: The Study of Drama Culture*
by LI Qiang
translated by GAO Fen

Vol. 2   *China's Belt and Road: The Initiative and Its Financial Focus*
by YU Xugang, Cristiano RIZZI, Mario TETTAMANTI,
Fabio E. ZICCARDI and GUO Li

Vol. 1   *The Political Economy of China's Belt and Road Initiative*
by ZOU Lei
translated by ZHANG Zhiping

Series on China's Belt and Road Initiative – Vol. 6

The Belt and Road Initiative in the
Global Context

Edited by

WANG Linggui
ZHAO Jianglin

Chinese Academy of Social Sciences, China

We World Scientific

EW JERSEY · LONDON · SINGAPORE · BEIJING · SHANGHAI · HONG KONG · TAIPEI · CHENNAI · TOKYO

Published by

World Scientific Publishing Co. Pte. Ltd.

5 Toh Tuck Link, Singapore 596224

USA office: 27 Warren Street, Suite 401-402, Hackensack, NJ 07601

UK office: 57 Shelton Street, Covent Garden, London WC2H 9HE

Library of Congress Cataloging-in-Publication Data

Names: Wang, Linggui, editor. | Zhao, Jianglin, editor.

Title: The Belt and Road Initiative in the global context / edited by:
    Linggui Wang (Chinese Academy of Social Sciences, China) and
    Jianglin Zhao (Chinese Academy of Social Sciences, China).

Description: New Jersey : World Scientific, [2019] | Series: Series on
    China's Belt and Road Initiative, vol. 6.

Identifiers: LCCN 2018056448 | ISBN 9789813277243 (hc : alk. paper)

Subjects: LCSH: Trade routes--Eurasia. | China--Foreign economic relations. |
    China--International cooperation. | International Symposium of the Belt
    and Road Initiative in the Global Perspective (2016 : Beijing, China)

Classification: LCC HF1604.Z4 B45 2019 | DDC 382/.30951--dc23

LC record available at https://lccn.loc.gov/2018056448

British Library Cataloguing-in-Publication Data

A catalogue record for this book is available from the British Library.

Sponsored by B&R Book Program

For any available supplementary material, please visit
https://www.worldscientific.com/worldscibooks/10.1142/11183#t=suppl

Desk Editors: Anthony Alexander/Lixi Dong

Typeset by Stallion Press
Email: enquiries@stallionpress.com

Preface

For the best part of several years, the Belt and Road (B&R) Initiative has gained growing interest in the form of the "Silk Road Economic Belt" and "21st Century Maritime Silk Road." Dating back to 7 September 2013, Xi Jinping, General Secretary of the Communist Party of China Central Committee and President of the People's Republic of China, delivered a speech titled "Promote People-to-People Friendship and Create a Better Future" in Kazakhstan, during which he proposed to "jointly build a Silk Road Economic Belt." On the following 3 October, President Xi gave a speech to Indonesia's parliament titled "Building China–ASEAN Community of Common Destiny" and introduced the proposal to "jointly build 21st Century Maritime Silk Road." Ever since then, scholars home and abroad started to explore how this initiative influences the world from their own countries' perspectives. As for our scholars, those from the National Institute for Global Strategy (NIGS), Chinese Academy of Social Sciences (CASS) focus more on joint study with scholars abroad to provide intellectual support for the B&R Initiative.

Today, nobody denies that the present global economy in general is in a downturn, with the major economies struggling in the limbo between revival and decline. Meanwhile, economic globalization is facing growing obstruction, in the form of fatigue drive of sustainable development, ceaseless regional conflicts, incessant regional hotspots, prevailing terrorism, and confrontation and alignment. Behind the challenges lie the international configuration and world order featured by emerging unequal and imbalanced development. Confronting these challenges is one mission shouldered by countries along the Belt and Road, and it will also be the way out for global issues. During the transitional period when international configuration and world order are restructuring and shifting intensely, the methods to advance sustainable development further strengthen and improve global governance, and maintain world peace and stability, urging deeper communication and cooperation.

China is now ready for in-depth interaction with the world and in-depth opening-up. Sailing down the stream of history, the construction of the B&R Initiative is one of the development strategies that Chinese government formulated for the 13th Five-Year Plan and the years ahead. The advancement of this construction is the requirement for China to integrate in the world more deeply. Furthermore, it is needed by countries around the world that seek codevelopment, especially Asian, African, and European countries. Therefore, the joint study is another attempt and exploration for "building think tanks with international perspective and improving international cooperation and communication mechanism." Jointly discussing the challenges faced by the development of the B&R Initiative will help us broaden our perspectives and tackle these challenges. We hope that domestic and foreign think tanks can build a better mutual understanding and support each other along the way of the B&R construction, thus paving the road for codevelopment.

Against such background, the NIGS of the CASS and Beijing Foreign Studies University (BFSU) held the "International Symposium of the Belt and Road Initiative in the Global Perspective" in the fall of 2016 in Beijing. After the Symposium, attendees home and abroad carried out an in-depth study of the subject discussed. This monograph is finished based on further study, which is also a phased outcome of the joint study conducted by the NIGS and major foreign think tanks.

Experts who are involved in the joint study generally believe that the B&R Initiative is China's grand strategy on expanding and deepening openingup to the world, building new pattern of reform and opening-up, achieving globalization 2.0 and fulfilling win–win cooperation. The Initiative has borne remarkable fruit in areas from top-level design and policy communication to facility-sharing, clearing trade channel, accommodation of funds, and common aspiration of people, thus forming coconsultation, coconstruction, and sharing among engaged countries. It has also broken new ground in terms of motivating the development of countries and regions along the route and exploiting huge potential for mutual development. Conforming to the inherent law of international economic development and actively accommodating the new trend of global economic cooperation, this initiative has drawn broad international consensus and attention for promoting global economy and has been referred to as the "Chinese prescription" to treat the global economy disease and the "Chinese plan" to solve current issues.

Indeed, while experts who participate in the study gave credit to the B&R Initiative, they also agreed that above the interconnection, coconsultation, coconstruction, and sharing, the most crucial and the most fundamental is the bonding of idea, where think tanks, a valuable treasure of a country, play an important role. At all times, rulers value the function of think tanks and see them as an important source for decision-making. Ever since the 18th National Congress of the Communist Party of China, the CPC Committee lead by General Secretary Xi Jinping has attached great importance to the development of think tanks and introduced major strategic measures to promote the position and function of think tanks in governance and diplomacy. On 12 November 2013, the Third Plenary Session of the 18th Central Committee of the CPC passed "Decision of the Central Committee of the Communist Party of China on Some Major Issues Concerning Comprehensively Deepening the Reform", in which the idea "to enhance the construction of new types of think tanks with Chinese characteristics and promote a consultative policy system" was put forward. On 20 January 2015, Chinese government issued "Opinions on Strengthening the Construction of New Think Tank with Chinese Characteristics." On 9 November of the same year, during the 18th Meeting of the Central Leading Group for Deepening Reform, "The National High-level Think Tank Building Pilot Project" was approved and 25 national high-level think tank pilot units were appointed. Also, the general requirements for high-level think tanks are put forward as follows: maintain high-end position, highlight professional characteristics, and innovate theories and policies; strengthen the application and orientation of subjects and initiate targeted and proactive policy studies, and the directions and the focal points of the studies must be derived from the major strategies deployed during the Fifth Plenum of the 18th Central Committee of the Communist Party of China.

Being one of the units, NIGS under CASS is also one of the two think tanks that focuses on global strategy, with its secretariat located at the National Institute of International Strategy, CASS. As for the leadership team, Professor Cai Fang is the Chairman of Board of Directors of NIGS, CASS. He is also the Vice President of CASS as well as the Member of the Chinese Academy of Social Sciences. Senior Diplomat and Ambassador Fu Ying, also the Director of the Foreign Affairs Committee of the NPC Standing Committee, possesses the title of Chief Expert of our think tank. Since its establishment, NIGS has focused on the study of the B&R Initiative, global strategy, and China's peripheral security. Engaging in academic exchanges and communications with domestic and foreign think tanks, the members are dedicated to replenish the theoretical support and decision reference for the implementation and advancement of the B&R Initiative.

Wang Linggui
Senior Research Fellow, Executive Vice Chairman of
Board of Directors & Secretary General of
National Institute for Global Strategy (NIGS),
Chinese Academy of Social Sciences

About the Editors

Wang Linggui Senior Research Fellow, Executive Vice Chairman of Board of Directors & Secretary General of National Institute for Global Strategy (NIGS), Chinese Academy of Social Sciences (CASS) since the end of 2015. His major study covers China's belt and road, China's global strategy, counter-terrorism issue, Middle East issue, and others. During the period of his position, he published about 400 pieces of papers, books and reports. Some of his works were awarded by CASS and some government institutions. He also acts as the chief of several important governmental study projects.

Zhao Jianglin Senior Research Fellow, Deputy Secretary of National Institute for Global Strategy (NIGS), Chinese Academy of Social Sciences (CASS). Her research areas cover International Economics, China's Belt and Road Initiative, and others. During the period of her position, she has published papers, books and reports and also acts as the chief of study projects.

Contents

Part 1

Challenges and Opportunities Faced by the Belt and Road Initiative

CHAPTER 1

The Belt and Road Initiative: Challenges, Cooperation, and Action

Wang Linggui and Zhao Jianglin

National Institute for Global Strategy,
Chinese Academy of Social Sciences, Beijing, China

1.1 Introduction

On 10 and 11 October 2016, the Symposium on the Belt and Road (B&R) Initiative in the Global Perspective was held in Beijing, jointly organized by the National Institute of Global Strategy (NIGS) of the Chinese Academy of Social Sciences (CASS) and Beijing Foreign Studies University (BFSU). Discussions on topics about the new global situation and challenges confronting the construction of the B&R, the multidisciplinary cooperation correlated to the B&R Initiative, and the solutions and suggestions to the promotion of the B&R Initiative were held with 31 foreign representatives from Russia, Egypt, Pakistan, US, Malaysia, Turkey, Singapore, India, and other 22 countries and 39 experts from China. At the opening ceremony, speeches were delivered by Mr. Cai Fang, an academician and a research fellow, Vice President of the CASS, and Director of NIGS; Mr. Masood, Pakistani Ambassador to China; Mr. Liew Chin Tong, Malaysia Congressman; Mr. Huang Ping, research fellow, and Director of the Europe Institute of CASS; and Peng Long, President of BFSU.

The agenda of the conference is discussed in the following sections.

1.2   The B&R Initiative: New Route to Promoting Version 2.0 of Globalization

At present, "anti-globalization" seems to be a prevailing trend. There are quite a few factors that lead to this consequence, such as the long-term slumps of the global economy, continuous regional conflicts, and disastrous aftermath of terrorism. All the above factors have led to a sharp drop in the enthusiasm of the developed countries toward global issues. In this background, the birth of the B&R Initiative is definitely a positive response to "anti-globalization". Hereby, the experts at the conference agree the following:

First, the B&R Initiative is a grand strategy for China to expand its opening-up policy, to establish a new pattern of open development, to forge version 2.0 of globalization, and to put the win–win cooperation concept into practice.

- The American scholars believe that it is China that has brought the new changes in world geopolitics and geoeconomics, and that China is becoming a very important power in globalization, which would bring revolutionary influence on global affairs.
- The Indian scholars believe that the B&R Initiative is a framework of geoculture instead of geopolitics and the Silk Road Economic Belt could be regarded as the second globalization initiated by the oriental world. At present, the Silk Road Economic Belt covers 63% of the world population, which represents 29% of the global GDP. The GDP ratio could be increased to 50% if the concepts of Make In India, Indian necklace along Himalayas, and India coastal necklace are connected to the B&R Initiative and if the Eurasian Economic Union initiative could be docked with the B&R Initiative.
- The Chinese scholars proposed to put the B&R Initiative in the background of the transforming global role. The multiple power

structure of the B&R Initiative should be strengthened to produce an everlasting power that is classified phase by phase. From the perspective of the free trade zone, some Chinese scholars believe that the pilot free trade zone is version 2.0 of the opening-up policy that is initiated by China in the current international situation. It is a grand strategy of synchronized integration at home and abroad. It represents the participation of China in formulating the new rules for international trade.

Second, the B&R Initiative has achieved significant accomplishments for the last three years in different aspects, such as its top design, policy communication, facilities connectivity, unimpeded trade, financial integration, and people-to-people bond. A cooperation environment of discussion, work, and sharing among different countries is cultivated.

- The Russian scholars believe that the B&R Initiative is in line with the regional and global trend of development. The B&R Initiative is not weakening or eliminating the current economy system. Instead, it represents the desire for peace, mutual benefit, and exchange of the international community. It helps promote free trade and fair cooperation, which is in the interest of all the countries. The realization of docking should be encouraged between the B&R Initiative and the Eurasian Economic Union, which has been advocated by Russia.
- The Indian scholars believe that China is promoting the B&R Initiative through the pattern of geoeconomics. The geopolitics and the geoeconomics should be related in the future. In other words, India should dock its own development strategy with the B&R Initiative.
- The Philippine scholars believe that the B&R Initiative of China is an international strategy. All the participating countries can relate it with their own national development projects. The Philippines is also very willing to actively participate in the construction of the B&R Initiative advocated by China.
- The Chinese scholars also put forward that the B&R Initiative is actually a major adjustment of China's opening-up policy and a readjustment of China's layout of its geoeconomics. The B&R Initiative

is mainly one of developing westward and opening to the developing countries.

Third, the B&R Initiative is transforming from a "China initiative" into a global action in the past three years. For the past few years, the B&R Initiative has complied with the inherent international law of economy development, adapted actively to the new trend of global economic cooperation, reached broad international consensus, and won the world's attention in the process of revitalizing the global economy. Therefore, it has been recognized as the "China prescription" for the current international economic and financial epidemic, and the "China approach" to solve the present problem.

- The Egyptian scholars look forward to more personnel exchanges with China and other countries. The ascension of political stability in Egypt would allow the country to play an important role in China's B&R Initiative by connecting Asia, Europe, and Africa.
- Sri Lanka actively supports the construction of the B&R Initiative because the initiative is in line with the development vision of the country. Relying on its own geographic advantage in the Indian Ocean, Sri Lanka could become a key hub on the Maritime Silk Road.
- The Kazakhstan scholars believe that the B&R Initiative can strengthen trade and economic cooperation between Kazakhstan and other countries to improve regional integration.
- The Indonesian scholars believe that the development strategy and vision of their country are a close fit to the B&R Initiative.
- Laos fully supports the B&R Initiative and aims at breaking away from the poverty caused by being a landlocked nation and obtaining economic development.
- Japanese scholars believe that the railway brings positive impact to all the relevant countries including Russia.
- By all means, the Malaysian scholars do not want to see the B&R Initiative as a game for interests between the big powers. Instead, it will bring us a new world if healthy free trade can promote peace of the world.

1.3 Challenges Facing the B&R Initiative: The General and Specific Risks

The participating experts at the conference generally believe that the B&R Initiative is transforming from the stage of conceptual explanation and publicity toward that of practical directions. In general, the major existing and potential risks and challenges are as follows:

(a) **Security risks:** There are three main categories: competition of power strategy hedges against the B&R Initiative; regional conflicts; terrorism and other non-traditional security threats.
(b) **Political risks:** There are also three main categories of political instability: color revolution; regime change; and secession.
(c) **Economic risks:** The B&R Initiative gives priority to economic projects. As an economic initiative, the B&R Initiative contains financing risks, credit risks for execution of contracts, profit return risks, and technical risks in the infrastructure construction.
(d) **Ecological risks:** The area that the B&R Initiative covers includes basically ecologically fragile regions. The infrastructure construction would bring certain threats to local ecological system.
(e) **Social risks:** Ethnic and tribal contradictions, religious, sectarian, and cultural conflicts, international crimes, drugs, epidemic diseases, etc. can turn to deadlock against the progress of the B&R Initiative.

Besides the general types of challenges, the B&R Initiative also faces specific problems in different countries.

- The Indian scholars discussed the reason why there were no enthusiastic responses from them during the discussion. First, the B&R Initiative was just brought up, and India was watching the actions and effects of the B&R Initiative. Second, India is taking some regions of the area as its own backyard. Third, there are traditional and non-traditional security risks. Fourth, India is concerned that the B&R Initiative may affect the stability of its northeastern area. Fifth, India is worried that China might form encirclement around India through the Maritime Silk Road. Besides, the China–India trade deficit also caused concern for India.

- The Pakistani scholars refuted the suspicions from the Indian scholars about the construction of the China–Pakistan Economic Corridor (CPEC). The CPEC is a cooperative practice between China and Pakistan. Pakistan does not need approval from India on whether it can carry out cooperation with any other countries.
- The Burmese scholars believe that the B&R Initiative is a kind of game-changing initiative, after comparing it with the World Bank, the AIIB, and the Bretton Woods System. The Chinese scholars believe that the B&R Initiative is improving and complementing the rules of the world trade system instead of changing the rules.
- The Sri Lankan scholars brought up the problem of the loan standard for the B&R Initiative. This would affect the operation of capital, which would further affect the overall progress of the B&R Initiative.
- The Afghan scholars put forward that the B&R construction should avoid the four mistakes that happened in the construction of Afghanistan with the US involvement. First, it should not leave Afghanistan highly dependent on foreign aid. Instead, economic development should rely on investment. Second, there should be emphasis on fight against terrorist militarism. Third, it should rely on regional participants. Fourth, it should work on regional consensus, and improve sustainable development.
- The scholars from the Central Asian countries believe that the countries in Central Asia should fully understand that China is a very important partner for economic cooperation in the region. The leaders of China and Russia should participate in the regional construction in a constructive way. Shanghai Cooperation Organization (SCO) did not fulfill its mission fully. With the annual budget of $4 billion, the result is not very obvious; therefore, China and Russia should carry out new cooperation under the frame of the B&R Initiative. The transparency issue should be given more attention. The infrastructure projects should not be taken as means for personal gains.
- As a third party, the Korean scholars put forward that China should pay attention to the concerns of the countries on its periphery. For example, countries that have conflicts with China on the South China

Sea worry that the construction of the Maritime Silk Road might collide with their territorial sovereignty and interests.

1.4 People-to-People Bond Equally Important as Infrastructure Construction

The seminar highly stressed the importance of people-to-people bond and regarded it as equally important as the construction of the infrastructure. In the past, foreign experts paid more attention to the construction of the "hardware" aspects of the B&R Initiative, the infrastructure. Today, people regard the software of the B&R Initiative as a key area, many experts expressed that the people-to-people bond is critical to the B&R.

First, people-to-people bond is particularly important to the B&R Initiative. Experts generally believe that people-to-people bond is an important component of the B&R Initiative. Chinese scholars believe that mutual understanding in culture can positively affect economic cooperation. The lack of a profound and mutual understanding in each other's social culture and traditions can most likely lead to failure of cooperation.

- The Russian scholars believe that soft power is a right to exert influence, the implementation of a common value shared by all communities in the society, and certain political and diplomatic strategies. The implementation of soft power strategy is to break these national, social, and cultural biases to support cultural progress to promote dialogue and exchange between different cultures.
- The Malaysian scholars believe that people-to-people bond includes mutual recognition and a harmonious friendly relationship between the peoples.
- The Pakistani scholars put forward that the personnel exchange and people-to-people bond are the key to the success of the B&R Initiative.

Second, certain problems in the field of people-to-people bond should not be ignored.

- The Malaysian scholars believe that the major problem for Southeast Asia in their study on China lies in the language. The Chinese research papers that most researchers from Southeast Asia need for reference are published in Chinese language, while the researches on China by western scholars are more easily accessible. The western scholars obtain lots of influence, while Chinese scholars might have academic exchanges with their counterparts in Southeast Asia more on personal basis. In reverse, for the study on Southeast Asia, China lacks experts who are familiar with the local languages of Southeast Asia. The research on Southeast Asia is still an interdisciplinary subject in China. Nevertheless, there are also problems for the Southeast Asian countries in their study of China.

- The Indian scholars believe that there is a mutual trust deficit between China and India, mainly due to inadequate understanding of each other's culture and civilization.
- The Chinese scholars stressed the importance of the people-to-people bond. Compared to its knowledge of the Christian civilization and the western world, China is lagging behind in its understanding of the Islamic world, the maritime civilization, and the underdeveloped regions in Eurasia.

Third, the construction of people-to-people bond should be strengthened in the future. The Kyrgyz scholars proposed that as the economic development strategy should be widely recognized, it must have popular support. The communication between the people of China and Kyrgyzstan needs to be enhanced.

For the construction of the people-to-people bond in the future, the Chinese scholars proposed that the academia should further explore the research in the docking of the civilizations and cultures of the countries along the B&R.

1.5 Expectations and Suggestions on the Future Construction of the B&R by the Scholars from Different Countries

The B&R is a grand initiative with global, long-term, and profound influence. The experts at the symposium produced valuable opinions and suggestions on the future construction of the B&R from various perspectives, which manifested anticipation for the fruitful results that would be brought by the B&R Initiative.

Some specific aspects are discussed in the following sections.

1.5.1 *Comprehensive Suggestions*

- First, the discussion of the B&R Initiative should be continued and strengthened. Communication and discussion will be helpful for the multilateral implementation of the B&R Initiative.
- Second, a roadmap and detailed plan of the B&R Initiative should be laid out, so that the localities in countries along the B&R could participate in its construction.
- Third, market orientation should be focused on, and the market operation should be emphasized. The Chinese scholars suggested that the government is playing a larger role at present in the construction of the B&R. While in the future, it should be transformed toward the enterprises.
- Fourth, the premise to the success of the B&R Initiative should be emphasized. The scholars from Korea suggested that the financial market as well as the technical assistance should be further open to win over support from the international organizations.
- Fifth, the key areas of the B&R construction should be highlighted. Internationally, the transportation across Europe and Asia should, first of all, be thoroughly achieved by high-speed rail. Domestically, the emphasis should be directed to the connection of the best route through the land and the sea.
- Sixth, the B&R Initiative should achieve the integration inside and outside of the country. A coordinated development should be implemented between the B&R Initiative and the Yangtze River economic belt strategy; the docking should also be strengthened between the B&R Initiative and the regional economic cooperation mechanisms, including the Eurasian Union, the SCO, the ASEAN, and the GCC.
- Seventh, bring the US into the B&R Initiative. The US dollar is the major currency of the world, the AIIB is operating over the US dollars rather than the RMB, and the US should belong to the B&R Initiative.

1.5.2 *Specific Countries and Regions*

1.5.2.1 Cooperation between China and India

The Chinese scholars suggested that the China–India cooperation should focus on the following areas:

- First, establish production capacity cooperation mechanisms.
- Second, actively promote the establishment of a free trade area, accelerate the construction of connectivity, and improve the investment environment.
- Third, confirm the priority areas of cooperation.
- Fourth, enhance cooperation in the financial sector. Make full use of the BRICS bank, the AIIB, and the Silk Road Fund to promote production capacity cooperation.
- Fifth, improve the level of mutual trust. Both China and India should not set up protective barriers against each other and prevent the rise from investment behavior to political security behavior.

The Indian scholars suggested that China and India should establish a coordinated mechanism. The B&R Initiative should not be the counterpart version of the Marshall Plan.

1.5.2.2 Cooperation between China and the Arabian Countries/the Middle East

The Chinese experts put forward several suggestions: actively promote the communication of policies between China and the Arabian countries; implement country-specific policies; vigorously promote the project of people-to-people bond.

Some experts proposed for a number of areas for cooperation: expand cooperation in the field of oil and gas to create an energy security community; carry out diversified financial cooperation to boost the internationalization process for the RMB.

1.5.3 *Specific Areas*

- First, the planning for the infrastructure interconnectivity should consider how to speed up the development of the periphery regions.

- Second, build a new economic corridor. The Nepali scholars believe that currently, there is a lack of connectivity between China, ASEAN, and South Asia. The ERIA is a circular economic corridor to improve the common prosperity of China and India. Whether China will consider participating in it remains uncertain.
- Third, intensify the cooperation in the manufacturing industry of the international production capacity equipment and achieve multilateral benefits. In this respect, attention should be paid to the following aspects: clarify the role that we play; provide production capacity of premium quality; avoid pollution of the environment and build a green silk road together.
- Fourth, intensify the understanding of the labor market in the countries along the B&R Initiative.
- Fifth, enhance educational cooperation. Some countries put a new premium on the role of education to the construction of the B&R. Currently, Cambodia has established a number of education cooperation agencies relevant to China.
- Sixth, let the border regions play their roles. Many residents of different ethnicities in the border areas are living across national borders. They can play the role of a bridge in the foreign economic exchange activities of China.

1.5.4 *Specific Measures*

- First, control various kinds of risks for the B&R Initiative. The Chinese experts put forward the following: setup of a benign mechanism of mutual benefit and mutual governance; setup of a mechanism of international financial and capital cooperation; integration of the B&R Initiative into the development planning of the UN, of the local organization, and of the host country; building risk database and making risk predictions.
- Second, emphasize the flexibility of the cooperation. The economic development level of some countries along the B&R Initiative is not very high, so it is not suitable for them to promote trade liberalization. China should strengthen the study on the flexibility of cooperation.

- Third, establish and intensify the institutionalization of docking. The construction process of the B&R Initiative should be from the docking of projects to the docking of systems. The failure rate of China's overseas investment is high, close to 90%, while the failure rate of the overseas mergers and acquisitions investment by Japan, US, and France is only about 30%. The main reason is that the Chinese companies work more on project docking without establishing a set of rules of bilateral and multilateral trade cooperation.
- Fourth, intensify the docking of the security systems. The political situation of many countries along the B&R is unstable. The security for the Chinese enterprises there cannot depend entirely on the security companies in these countries. The Chinese security companies should also operate abroad.
- Fifth, build schools in the peripheral countries to improve the quality of the labor force; meanwhile, cultivate friendly feelings to China in the younger generation.
- Sixth, make plans for the construction of the communication platform for the B&R Initiative by strengthening the cooperation between media agencies, setting up certain subjects for publicity, and making good publicity work abroad for the B&R Initiative.
- Seventh, intensify research, such as focusing on the economic benefits by studying from the perspective of the comprehensive benefits that are produced by the B&R Initiative. The B&R Initiative is an economic initiative advocated by China, but it will definitely bring a series of political, social, and security benefits.
- Eighth, the issue of the discourse power is significant in the construction of the B&R Initiative. How to handle the leadership for public opinions together with the countries along the B&R and build the discourse power together is a subject for research and discussion in the course of the B&R construction.
- Ninth, the Burmese scholars proposed that China should strengthen the cooperation with the World Bank, the AIIB, and the IMF, and learn from their project experience.
- Tenth, increase consensus in the course of the project landing to intensify the solid sense of gain by the people at the periphery regions.

- Eleventh, achieve good translation work for the classics. Translate the Chinese literature into Southeast Asian languages and encourage Chinese students to do research in Southeast Asia.

1.5.5 *"Seven Suggestions": Put into Practice the Communication of Ideas*

Either for connectivity, or for discussion together, construction together, and sharing together, the most essential component is the communication of ideas, in which the think tanks play a vital role.

As an important component of the people-to-people bond, the communication and cooperation between think tanks play a very important role in guiding the national policy and improving the public consciousness. The NIGS should make differences in the construction of the B&R in the future. Hereby, Mr. Wang Linggui, Executive Vice Chairman of Board of Directors & Secretary of the NIGS under CASS, put forward the following seven suggestions:

- First, work together to pick up a number of research topics about the B&R Initiative. The B&R Initiative is a big subject, from which every expert from every think tank can select topics from his or her own field of research and could also provide significant guide to the construction of the B&R and response to thc concerns of the various countries in the world.
- Second, carry out joint research on certain major issues. Every think tank has its own specialty and field of research. The joint research can produce positive contribution to the construction of the B&R.
- Third, establish an information system of sharing the results. An information-sharing system should be set up as a common foundation and step of the research.
- Fourth, train talents together. Personnel exchanges among the participating think tanks are suggested.
- Fifth, host conferences together. Conference is the place where ideas are brought together. The conference is also the place to put people-to-people bond into practice. Participating in the conference together is helpful for better communication and for reaching consensus.

- Sixth, publish joint phasic or thematic reports. The think tanks can periodically publish joint reports of researches on subjects which would produce positive impact on the society and on the decision-making of the country.
- Seventh, set up a common contact mechanism. Each think tank may designate its daily contact personnel and set up its daily contact regulations.

To the above "seven suggestions", the participating experts have made positive responses. Some of them offered to welcome Chinese scholars to station at and study in their institutes in order to improve the interaction between the Chinese and overseas institutions and to promote the local recognition of the B&R Initiative; some of them proposed creation of an essay collection out of the proceedings of this symposium as a result-sharing mechanism; some of them suggested strengthening of translation; and some others suggested set up of websites and databases for the conference.

CHAPTER 2

The Belt and Road Initiative: Why Globalization Drives in Asia and Beyond Need to be Integrated?

Bali Ram Deepak

Center of Chinese and Southeast Asian Studies,
Jawaharlal Nehru University, New Delhi, India

2.1 The Development of the Belt and Road Initiative

Ever since the Belt and Road (B&R) Initiative has been proposed by President Xi Jinping, it has evoked hopes as well as suspicions across continents. Even if silk routes existed in ancient times, what is the relevance of such initiatives in modern times? Also, are such initiatives in sync with China's foreign policy goals, such as multipolarity, despising hegemony, common security, and other similar notions, or is the initiative an antidote to the US foreign policy goals like "pivot to Asia" or "Trans-Pacific Partnership Agreement" (TPP)? Or, is China challenging the US hegemony and rewriting the rules of global geopolitical and economic architecture?

Undoubtedly, the B&R Initiative is rooted in history, as there was an overland Silk Route and a Maritime Silk Route (MSR) that connected China to countries across Asia, Africa, and Europe. In the last three decades of reforms, China built a network of highways and railroads from north to south and from east to less developed western and southwestern regions. Having achieved that, China sees an opportunity to link the hinterland with South Asia, Europe, Africa and even the Americas by revitalizing the ancient channels of communion and commerce.

The concept was first proposed by Xi Jinping during a speech at Nazarbayev University, Kazakhstan on 7 September 2013 when he said that "To forge closer economic ties, deepen cooperation, and expand development in the Euro-Asia region, we should take an innovative approach and jointly build an 'economic belt' along the silk road. This will be a great undertaking benefitting the people of all countries along the route." Xi proposed that traffic connectivity will need to be improved so as to open the strategic regional thoroughfare from the Pacific Ocean to the Baltic Sea, and gradually move toward the setting up of a network of transportation that connects Eastern, Western, and Southern Asia. President Xi Jinping also urged the regional members to promote local-currency settlement so as to improve their immunity to financial risks and their global competitiveness.[1] Undoubtedly, the economic connectivity is the heart of the matter for which President Xi Jinping also announced the establishment of a Silk Road Fund with US$ 40 billion to support infrastructure investments in countries involved; however, the notion is equally significant strategically as it will imply common security or security dilemmas at regional and trans-regional levels.

The initiative of building the 21st Century MSR was proposed by Xi Jinping during his visit to Indonesia in October 2013 in order to deepen economic and maritime links. The MSR begins in Fuzhou in Southeast China's Fujian province and heads south into the ASEAN nations, crosses Malacca Strait and turns west to countries along the Indian Ocean before meeting the land-based Silk Road in Venice via the Red Sea and Mediterranean Sea. Under the ambit of MSR, China plans to build hard and soft infrastructure from the Indo-Pacific region to Africa, including transport, energy, water management, communication, earth monitoring, economic and social infrastructure. The B&R Initiative

---

[1] "Xi suggests China, C. Asia build Silk Road Economic Belt" 7 September 2013 Xinhua News. Wang Yiwei, *The Belt and Road Initiative: What will China offer the World in its Rise* (New World Press, Beijing, 2016).

advocates policy communication, infrastructure connectivity, unimpeded trade, monetary circulation, and people-to-people relations. Some scholars have added a sixth element to it — interconnected network or the internet silk road thus making the notion as One Belt Two Roads.

2.2 Why is the B&R Initiative an Opportunity?

China has sought the participation of countries and regions touching the B&R zone. For example, most of the ASEAN countries with which China has a trade volume of over 400 billion dollars have welcomed the idea. As far as South Asia is concerned, except India most of the smaller nations have also welcomed the idea as they perceive the initiative as a great opportunity to comprehensively deepen economic and people-to-people relations. As of date, 65 countries along the B&R Initiative are part of the project. These countries account for 63% of the world population but contribute only 29% to the world GDP, of which China alone accounts for over 50%. Therefore, it is indeed an opportunity for these countries, which are largely developing countries, and could push their economic growth and alleviate poverty.

China realizes the importance of the geoeconomic as well as geostrategic importance of the MSR, as there are 32 littoral countries including China that touch the 21st Century MSR. The combined population of these countries is around 4 billion people with a GDP of around US$ 21 trillion. These are the countries with huge potentials that have achieved rapid economic growth recently. From 2007 to 2012, the lowest annual growth rate was 5.27% that of Sudan, and the highest average annual growth rate was 22.83% that of Myanmar.[2] In view of these figures, China believes that the 21st Century MSR is going to be an important driver of regional as well as global economic growth. Given the over capacities and structural adjustments being carried out in China, also pronounced as "New Normal", China sees an opportunity for sustaining its domestic economy on the one hand while strengthening strategic partnership with various countries on the other.

---

[2]C. Wanlin and H. Chuantian, *Game between Parties and Economic Orientation of the Maritime Silk Road* (Regional Economy, Guang dong, 2014).

In the context above, the B&R Initiative is the reiteration of the geocivilization paradigm of the yesteryears, for it connects via land and sea the four major civilizations, such as Egypt, Babylon, China, and India, of which the latter two are the oldest yet living civilizations. The geocivilizational paradigm is an antidote to geopolitics of the present day led by the US that has divided the nations rather than uniting them, and we still witness the raging flames of war across continents even today. It is not, however, to say that there were no problems with the geocivilizational thinking, there were minor ones, but largely the concept remained anti-expansionist, one that casts off hegemony and preaches peaceful co-existence.

The B&R Action Plan released during the Boao Forum on Asia in Hainan in 2015 points out that economic connectivity is the heart of the matter for which Chinese President Xi Jinping also announced the establishment of a Silk Road Fund with US$ 40 billion to support infrastructure investments in countries involved, and has also linked the establishment of Asian Infrastructure Investment Bank (AIIB) and Brazil, Russia, India, China and South Africa (BRICS) New Development Bank to the initiative as well. Therefore, the B&R Initiative will also redefine the rules of global governance, where emerging economies like the BRICS along with others will have a bigger say in the institutions of global governance. The BRICS countries have been vocal in asking for greater representation in the global governance architecture for quite some time now. Unimpeded trade and monetary circulation could be guaranteed by these institutional mechanisms listed above.

The B&R Initiative rather than just "rebalancing to Asia" or a certain region, aims at global rebalancing where the "Silk Road Spirit" would be brought into full play. The B&R Initiative action plan has interpreted the "Silk Road Spirit" as the one that advocates "peace and cooperation, openness and inclusiveness, mutual learning and mutual benefit." It says that the initiative is in line with the purposes and principles of the UN Charter. The initiative is open and inclusive; former Chinese ambassador to India, Amb. Le Yucheng, does not subscribe it as a Chinese solo but as "a symphony performed by various countries." Therefore, the B&R Initiative will not only aim to realize the Chinese dream, but also the dreams of other countries along the Belt and Road. The B&R Initiative essentially is an antidote to the "China threat theory," "pivot to Asia," and other similar notions. Unlike the Marshal Plan that resulted in the creation of the NATO and Cold War, the B&R Initiative aims to create inclusiveness. Chinese scholars, including Prof. Shi Ze[3] of the China Institute of International Studies, have denounced the western criticism of the initiative and have maintained that the Three-Nos Policy — non-interference in the internal affairs of other nations; not to seek the so-called "sphere of influence"; and not to strive for hegemony or dominance — equally applies to the B&R Initiative. The initiative indeed is larger than the Marshall plan as it attempts to encompass the entire world, the economic value of which could reach whopping US$ 21 trillion.[4] Will this grandiose concept succeed and realize not only the Chinese dream but the dreams of various countries and people around the world? Or will it give rise to geostrategic rivalries around the world and cold or hot war with the sole and declining superpower of the world?

2.3 Old and New Globalization Forces

With increasingly intense globalization and interdependence, various regional economic blocks, such as Association of Southeast Asian Nations (ASEAN) in Southeast Asia, European Union (EU) in Europe, North American Free Trade Agreement (NAFTA) in North America, Mercado Común del Sur or Southern Common Market (MERCOSUR) in Latin America, South Asian Association for Regional Cooperation (SAARC) in South Asia, Eurasian Economic Union (EEU) sprawling across Russia and Central Asian Republics and many more at the subregional level have emerged all over the globe.

In Asia, the initiation of reforms and open-door policy in China especially since Deng Xiaoping's South China tour in 1992, Indian economic reforms in 1991 especially its "Look East Policy" (LEP), and a

---

[3] S. Ze, "One Road & One Belt" new thinking with regard to concepts and practice, *Lecture delivered at the 30th anniversary of Conference of the Schiller Institute,* 14 October, 2014, Germany, Available at http://newparadigm.schillerinstitute.com/media/one-road-and-one-belt-and-new-thinking-with-regard-to-concepts-and-practice/

[4] S. Tiezzi, The new silk road: China's Marshall Plan? *The Diplomat,* 6 November 2014. Available at http://thediplomat.com/2014/11/the-new-silk-road-chinas-marshall-plan/

similar opening from Bangladesh in the 1990s and Myanmar in late 1980s have created favorable conditions for further regional economic groupings and triggered trends of integration.

The B&R Initiative is mainly a globalization process that will spur domestic, regional as well as global economic growth. It is essentially a re-globalization drive from the east in the backdrop of the financial woes of the west and its increasingly protectionist tendencies of late. In the same vein, India, ever since Prime Minister Modi has ascended to the power, has also initiated a series of projects such as "Make in India", "Digital India", "Start-up India", "Sagarmala", "Bharatmala", etc. with global ramification.

We have witnessed that China immensely benefitted from the deep globalization of 1990s and 2000s, thus lifting millions of people from poverty. Can India and China integrate or dock their respective processes and create a new global economic ecosystem with deeper economic and political stakes? Or, should we allow building spheres of exclusive interests? Should we not move away from the Westphalian paradigm of security? Should we not argue in favor of "security with" as opposed to "security against" the adversary? Should we build a common economic, cultural, and security community in Asia?

I believe in the metamorphosis of both Indian and Chinese initiatives, which along with other similar initiatives will undoubtedly facilitate the integration of the region culturally, economically, and in the process help us to have a paradigm of common and collective security. However, why has India's response to the B&R Initiative remained so lackadaisical?

2.4 Why has India been so Lackadaisical?

Why has India remained silent to China's invitation even if the former has underscored the importance of India as far as the initiative is concerned? At the outset, India has expressed its unhappiness for not being consulted prior to the initiation of the B&R Initiative. Second, in the same vein, China without consulting India declared the Bangladesh–China–India–Myanmar Economic Corridor (BCIMEC) as part of the B&R Initiative which was signed way back during Premier Li Keqiang's India visit in 2013. Also, another corridor, the China–Pakistan Economic Corridor

(CPEC) that ran through the disputed territory claimed by India has caused serious concerns in India. Other four corridors that China announced as part of the B&R Initiative are China–Mongolia–Russia Economic Corridor (CMREC); New Eurasian Land Bridge (NELB); China–Central and West Asia Economic Corridor (CCWAEC); China–Indo-China Peninsula Economic Corridor (CICPEC). It is for these reasons that security analysts and sceptics in India see these initiatives as part of "strategic encirclement" of India along with the prospective Trans-Himalayan Economic Zone of Cooperation with Nepal and Bhutan, and hence the argument that India cannot give China access to its sensitive areas. Third, India which is embracing the US for security cooperation would not like to antagonize the US by joining China's bandwagon; it would rather tread a fine balancing line between the two. Having said that, is the Modi government thinking differently on the issue? It is, if we analyze the larger issue of regionalization and China's economic cooperation with India.

2.5 Should India be an Onlooker?

As far as the B&R Initiative of China is concerned, India has been part of the initiative with the signing of the BCIMEC. The work is in progress. As India's LEP has been widening in scope, this is an area where the policy could be integrated, especially when we are thinking of developing land-locked and underdeveloped northeastern region of India. India needs to take a leaf out of China's experience as to how it has developed and connected its southwestern and southern states to the ASEAN. Is New Delhi ready to forgo its sensitivities in Northeast in terms of economic development of the region? Can the massive trade between China–ASEAN and India–ASEAN percolate to the Northeast India and Northwest China? The answer to all these questions is yes provided we start looking at boundaries as gateways but not barriers.

In the same vein, India and China could think of developing similar corridors along the northwestern regions of China, primarily Xinjiang and Tibet, with India's Jammu and Kashmir, and the plains of Bihar and Uttar Pradesh intersecting Nepal. Boao Forum B&R Action Plan defines Xinjiang as a core area both politically and geographically. China considers Xinjiang as a window to the west and Central, South, and West Asia.

Both the medium- and long-term goals have been in place to realize the B&R Initiative. South Asia, I believe, is not just the CPEC which according to the Action Plan is medium-term goal aimed at completing railway and road connectivity between China and Pakistan within 5–10 years. Long-term goals are set to be achieved by the year 2049. These goals are Three Channels, Three Bases, and Five Centers in Xinjiang. Three Channels include North–Central–Southern Channels; Three Bases comprise oil & gas, coal and wind power bases; Five Centers are healthcare, traffic, culture, etc.

Several possibilities could be explored. An energy corridor could be established, which I believe will be more feasible and viable than the TAPI pipeline. Second, some of the nodes from CEPC could run southward and integrate the same with Chinese investment in Gujarat. This may prove another confidence building measure between India and China and may render India's Gwader dilemma irrelevant. Similarly, the Trans Himalayan railway cutting across Nepal and connecting India's prospective line in Nepal would be another option to explore.

As regards the 21st Century MSR, India has been responding by its own strategy. It has been expanding and strengthening its maritime partnerships with the United States, Japan, Vietnam, Australia, and other countries on the one hand, and engaging ASEAN in various domains on the other. Besides, there are new initiatives, such as "Project Mausam" initiated by the Ministry of Culture, in tandem with the Archaeological Society of India (ASI), New Delhi as the nodal agency and Indira Gandhi National Centre for the Arts (IGNCA), New Delhi as its Research Unit. Since the area covered under the project extends from East Africa, the Arabian Peninsula, the Indian subcontinent and Sri Lanka to the Southeast Asia, and has been termed as Indian Ocean "world", analysts and media have termed it as India's response to China's MSR. However, I believe, it is a pure cultural construct that does not pose any challenge, whatsoever to the B&R Initiative. Even if the "project" sounds ambitious, the kind of economic muscle which is required to materialize it simply does not exist. Contrary to this "project", the ambitious "Sagarmala" by way of which India desires to lay a network of rails, roads, smart cities, industrial parks, and high-speed rail along the east and west coasts of India is the area where Indian and Chinese initiatives could be integrated.

China has regarded India as an important country and crucial for economic integration in the region. China is already a partner in India's development; there is cooperation in the railway sector as regards enhancing the speed and heavy haul of the trains, China is also assisting India in the training of railway personnel, design of the stations, and in building up a railway university in India. The feasibility study of Delhi–Chennai high-speed railway has been going on and will bring down the travel time to 7 h from the present 28 h. There are mega plans to build industrial parks across India through the Chinese capital; the realtors from China have committed billions of dollars investment in Indian markets; telecom and energy sector of India has immensely benefitted from the Chinese investment. However, given the size and population of India and China, the investment and overall trade volume between the two remain very low. There is an upward movement this year, if the figures are to be believed, Chinese investment in India this year has reached an all-time high of US$ 700 million.

In this context, it would be unfortunate if India remains outside the value chain of such an initiative; however, it may decide for itself what kind of project it could carry out with China on case-to-case basis. These could be in the realm of a variety of infrastructure-related projects, including energy, transport, power, e-commerce, and projects integrating investment and trade. China will also perhaps frame its own responses and priorities toward countries along the Belt and Road. For example, it will have differentiated strategy while dealing with smaller and medium-sized countries, with conflicting parties in South China Sea, "pivot" countries like Pakistan and big and large countries like India.

Second, as India faces uncertainties as well as opportunities, it must capitalize on the invaluable geopolitical strategic space it has in the Indo-Pacific. If the US is attempting to offset China's geopolitical pull by way of India confronting China or in tandem with the US and its allies in the seas and land, it would be disastrous for all the stakeholders. From an Indian point of view, if the US is looking for a strong economic partnership with India, so is the case of India's economic engagement with China. It would be naive to say that the US will dump its interests in China for India. Imagine the $521 billion trade volume between China and the US and compare it with our trade with China and the US combine!

Therefore, if at all India would like to be a so-called "swing power" between China and the US, we need to be a swing power as far as cooperation and healthy competition and India's national interests are concerned not the confrontation and conflict, which is neither in India's interest nor in the interest of China and the US.

Finally, since the maritime ambitions of both India and China are soaring, the interests are overlapping too. There is an urgent need for initiating more comprehensive consultation mechanisms; one in the offing could be a substantive maritime security dialogue which has remained a non-starter since 2012; another could be a consultation mechanism on the B&R Initiative itself to explore the possibilities of docking the policies of the two countries in view of the initiatives having been taken to globalize their economies.

Further Reading

C. Dingding, China's 'Marshall Plan' is much more, *The Diplomat*, 10 November 2014. Available at http://thediplomat.com/2014/11/chinas-marshall-plan-is-much-more/.

Z. Shiping, *China's Sea Rights* (People's Daily Publication, Beijing, 2009).

CHAPTER 3

Deepening of Northeast Asia Economic Integration through the Belt and Road Initiative: A Korean Perspective

Hyung-Gon Jeong

*Korea Institute for International
Economic Policy, Sejong, South Korea*

3.1 Introduction

This chapter proposes ways to deepen Northeast Asia Economic integration through the Belt and Road (B&R) Initiative and other regional initiatives such as the Korean Eurasian Initiative.

3.2 The Chinese Economy: Background for the B&R Initiative

As we all know, the Chinese economy experienced rapid growth for a prolonged period, but a significant shift in its growth pattern occurred during the global financial crisis of 2008. During the six years leading up to 2007, China's GDP grew at an average rate of 11%, with investment equaling 41.5% of GDP. The current account surplus rose during this period, reaching more than 10% of GDP. In more than six years since the global crisis, however, the external surplus has fallen sharply into the range of 3% of GDP, but the shortfall in demand was made up almost completely by an increase in investment, which has reached more than 50% of GDP in recent years. China's growth has been impressive compared with the rest of the world, but the growth rate has slowed to around 7%, down to more than four percentage points from the pre-crisis period.[1] Thus, recently, China has been relying a lot more on investments to grow its economy — significantly more than in the past. China's response to this changing growth dynamic is partly external and partly internal.

3.3 China's Intensions

3.3.1 *Historical Background*

The old Silk Road is one of the main components of the B&R Initiative. The Silk Road was opened during China's Han dynasty and it commercially linked the regions of the ancient world throughout the Song and Ming dynasties (from the 10 through the 17 centuries). The Maritime Silk Road was established during the Ming Dynasty. The term "Silk Road" is representative of the most prosperous and liberal stage in Chinese history. It was also a stage or time when China's influence over the rest of the world was at its peak.

Throughout Chinese history, Chang'an (today, Xi'an), the capital of the Tang dynasty (7 to 10 century), was the most open city — also the largest city in the world. Chang'an was a cosmopolitan city with a large foreign population. Thus, Chang'an remains a symbol of openness. China, at the time, was a more liberal and open place than other countries in the world. It is not surprising that Xian, with its history of openness and international exchange, became the starting point of the B&R Initiative. At its heart, the B&R Initiative is a plan to help China realize an economic dream that started long ago.

---

[1]D. David, China's rise as a regional and global power: The AIIB and the 'one belt one road', Horizons, Brookings website. Available at https://www.brookings.edu/research/chinas-rise-as-a-regional-and-global-power-the-aiib-and-the-one-belt-one-road/ (accessed on 2 April 2017).

3.3.2 *Internal Motivations*

The B&R Initiative projects are part of China's internal strategy for a new engine for growth under a "new normal" economy, where the growth rate hovers around or below 7% — the plan is to encourage overseas investment and export. In addition, China's overcapacity in sectors, such as iron and steel, cement, and aluminum, is believed to be threatening the Chinese economy. China intends to resolve overproduction by expanding investment in infrastructure and by transferring production facilities overseas to countries along the B&R Initiative in railway.

In tandem with an economic slowdown, narrowing urban/rural disparity and securing energy supplies are the main concerns for the Chinese economy. To develop markets and promote investment in the underdeveloped regions of China, the B&R Initiative mainly focuses on infrastructure building and transportation supply chains in the western regions.

The B&R Initiative includes natural resources projects along the pipelines of the economic corridors. The corridors will open new routes to the Middle East as well as Central Asia. These corridors will provide an alternative route to the Gulf region through a Maritime Silk Road and increase accessibility to Central Asia through the overland pipelines of the Silk Road Economic Belt. This will render the supply of energy more secure and cost-effective.

3.3.3 *External Motivations*

China is attempting to take the lead in regional economic integration; it is doing so by exercising influence over neighboring countries through financing regional development projects. There is a consensus among observers that China is attempting to create a new order in the international political economy — an international political economy currently dominated by the US through its leading role in the World Trade Organization, World Bank, and International Monetary Fund. The B&R Initiative and the Asian Infrastructure Investment Bank (AIIB) jointly provide a platform for economic cooperation and help to further strengthen the interdependence between China and member countries (see Table 3.1). This was interpreted as a counter to the US-led Trans-Pacific

Table 3.1: AIIB Subscriptions and Voting Power of Member Countries.

Item	Member	Amount (million USD)	Share of subscriptions (%)	Total votes	Share of votes (%)
Regional					
1	China	29,780.4	34.67	301,031	29.90
2	India	8,367.3	9.74	86,900	8.63
3	Russia	6,536.2	7.61	68,589	6.81
4	Korea	3,738.7	4.35	40,614	4.03
5	Australia	3,691.2	4.30	40,139	3.99
6	Indonesia	3,360.7	3.91	36,834	3.66
7	Turkey	2,609.9	3.04	29,326	2.91
8	Saudi Arabia	2,544.6	2.96	28,673	2.85
9	Thailand	1,427.5	1.66	17,502	1.74
10	United Arab Emirates	1,185.7	1.38	15,084	1.50
Non-regional					
1	Germany	4,484.2	5.22	48,069	4.77
2	France	3,375.6	3.93	36,983	3.67
3	UK	3,054.7	3.56	33,774	3.35
4	Netherlands	1,031.1	1.20	13,540	1.34
5	Poland	831.8	0.97	11,545	1.15

Source: World Bank.

Partnership Agreement (TPP) and Transatlantic Trade and Investment Partnership (TTIP) pacts.

3.4 International Response to the B&R Initiative

From the beginning, the US response to the B&R Initiative has been unfavorable. Washington perceives it as a Chinese strategy to extend geographic influence and leverage over its neighbors, including US allies, through trade and investment practices. A White House statement from October 2015 states, "We can't let countries like China write the rules of the global economy."[2] The Japanese position is like that of the US. Although key NATO allies, such as France, the UK, and Germany, have joined China's AIIB, Japan has not.[3] Korea, on the other hand, perceives the B&R Initiative along with the China–Korea FTA as a major opportunity to reinforce interconnectivity with China and other Asian countries.

Major countries in ASEAN including Vietnam, Philippines, and Malaysia also joined the AIIB in 2016. These ASEAN member countries seek to balance relations with China and the United States. India has embraced the AIIB with the hope of receiving development finance to spur its growth. Also, with the second largest voting share in AIIB, India expects to play a key role in the China-led B&R Initiative and AIIB. Uzbekistan was among the first states to support the idea of the Silk Road Economic Belt. Uzbekistan expects that the B&R Initiative will strengthen mutually beneficial strategic partnerships and attract massive investments to develop national and regional infrastructure. Uzbekistan was the center of the ancient Silk Road, and Uzbeks today are interested in the revival of the Silk Road and in serving as a hub of the Silk Road once again. The B&R Initiative is seen to be in the interest of the entire Eurasian continent.

3.5 Deepening Economic Cooperation: The Eurasia Initiative and the B&R Initiative

The Eurasia Initiative is a concept proposed by the Korean President Park Geun-hye at the International Conference on Global Cooperation in the Era of Eurasia (18 October 2013). The main idea is to create employment and revitalize the economy through regional cooperation among Eurasian countries. It is also hoped that it might help alleviate tensions on the Korean peninsula and build a basis for reunification. The Eurasian Initiative proposes the creation and development of a single and unified system of transport, energy, and trade networks, along with

---

[2]The White House Website, Available at https://www.whitehouse.gov/the-press-office/2015/10/05/statement-president-trans-pacific-partnership.
[3]*The Economist*, Available at http://www.economist.com/news/asia/21652351-will-japan-lend-its-muscle-chinas-new-asian-infrastructure-bank-join-or-not-join

the implementation of economic cooperation and exchanges within the spheres of science, technology, and culture (including interpersonal relationships), as well as efforts to improve inter-Korean relations based on trust. This concept became official around the same time as the roll out of the B&R Initiative by Chinese President Xi Jinping. The Eurasia Initiative emphasizes an interactive, open, creative, and convergent Eurasia. The vision for the Eurasia Initiative can be summarized as: "One Continent, Creative Continent, and Peaceful Continent" (see Table 3.2).

The key partner countries for economic cooperation in Eurasia are China, Central Asian countries, Russia, Mongolia, and Turkey. They account for 25% of the total population and 19% of the world's trade volume. The Central Asian countries, Russia, and Mongolia are rich in resources but have weak industrial infrastructure. Korea and China, on the other hand, have a developed industry structure and high energy demand. This suggests a vast opportunity for regional cooperation in trade investment and technical cooperation. Intraregional trade structure remains unbalanced due to underdeveloped transportation and logistics networks and insufficient infrastructure in general, as well as uncertainty over investment, and insufficient cooperation. Despite their geographical importance, Central Asia, Mongolia, and the People's Republic of Korea are left out of intraregional trade due to factors such as underdeveloped

Table 3.2: The Eurasia Initiative Vision.

One continent	Establish complex logistics network linking Eurasia with railway and roads
	Materialize the Silk Road Express from Busan, crossing the DPRK, Russia, China, Central Asia, and Europe
	Strengthen the energy network of electricity, gas, pipelines, etc.
	Establish institutional frameworks such as the Regional Comprehensive Economic
	Partnership (RCEP) or the TPP to create a common market
Creative continent	Create new markets and employment by using and combining creativity-based science, technology and ICT
	Promote active personal and cultural exchanges within Eurasia
Peaceful continent	Strengthen regional peace and security through the Trust-Building Process on the Korean Peninsula and the Northeast Asia Peace and Cooperation Initiative

Source: Made by the author.

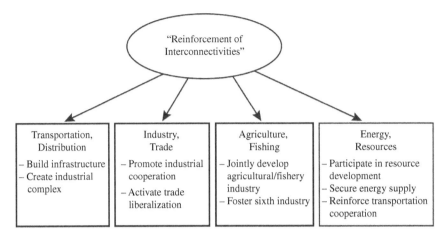

Figure 3.1: Roadmap for the Eurasia Initiative: Four Main Areas.

infrastructure. According to the World Bank Logistics Performance Index (LPI), five Central Asian countries are ranked 114th–149th (among 160 countries) in terms of LPI, while Russia ranks 90th and Mongolia is 135th. Specifically, these countries have a differing railway system standard which leads to difficulties in interconnection and higher cost of transport and they lag world standards in terms of technology development and management systems.

The Eurasia Initiative emphasizes the importance of interconnectivity among four main areas: transportation and distribution, industry and trade, agriculture and fisheries, energy and resources (see Figure 3.1). The Korean Initiative resembles the B&R Initiative which emphasizes "five connectivity": policy communication, financial integration, unimpeded trade, facilities connectivity, and people-to-people bond.

3.6 The B&R Initiative and Eurasia Initiative: The Need for China–Korea Cooperation

There is a need for China–Korea coordination to strengthen economic cooperation in Northeast Asia. The B&R Initiative and the Eurasia Initiative share the common goal of peace and economic development through cooperation in the region. Both China and Korea want political stability in the Korean peninsula and economic prosperity in Asia.

All countries share a common interest in the Central Asian region and in the development of China's three northeastern provinces. There is consensus between China and Korea over the desirability of reviving the ancient Silk Road as a major network. Chinese plans such as the "Revitalize the Old Northeast Industrial Bases" plan, the "Changjitu Project, and Hadaqi Industrial Corridor" plan are compatible with the Northeast Asian cooperation plans of Korea.

China–Korea cooperation in the implementation of the B&R Initiative and the Eurasia Initiative can propel the integration of Northeast Asia. These two concepts are expected to consolidate a strategic partnership between China and Korea based on a shared interest in creating an engine for economic growth and strengthening economic/diplomatic relations with neighboring countries. From a Korean perspective, the two countries can jointly exercise leadership to promote regional economic integration and the B&R Initiative stability and peace, as well as promote bilateral cooperation.

Factors such as common geographical coverage, shared goals (regional peace and stability), and shared interests in specific areas (such as cooperation on transportation and distribution networks and their interaction) will likely lead to a connection between the two concepts. For instance, the Eurasia Initiative includes building a complex distribution network linking Eurasian countries with railways and roads, while the B&R Initiative emphasizes building infrastructure and energy cooperation projects, namely, building natural gas pipelines between China and Central Asia (see Table 3.3).

The two initiatives have their respective strengths. The Korean Eurasia Initiative is strong in terms of information and communication technology (ICT) and in industries of the future and management know-how of global enterprises. The strengths of the B&R Initiative are overall industrial cooperation including investment in transportation/logistics infrastructure, ample funds and experience in various types of constructions, and wide intraregional networks based on past experiences.

The question emerges: How can these initiatives contribute positively to Northeast Asian integration? To facilitate Northeast Asian economic integration, hard and soft infrastructure must be built. As mentioned, China's B&R Initiative is perceived as a way to resolve its excess

Table 3.3: Comparison of the Eurasia Initiative and the B&R Initiative.

Eurasia Initiative (Korean Plan)	Belt and Road Initiative (Chinese Plan)
Comprehensive economic cooperation	Emphasis on 'connectivity' Connection between Silk Road Economic Bell and 21st century Maritime Silk Road
Industrial cooperation including ICT investment	Overall industrial cooperation including investment in transportation and logistics infrastructure (emphasis on five areas of connectivity)
ICT technology and leading role in future industry	Ample funds and experience in various types of construction
Management know-how of global enterprises	Efficient policy implementation by government
The most prominent candidate to induce opening of the DPRK's markets	Wide intraregional networks based on past experiences

Necessities of manufacturing industry base and supply of energy sources

Benefits from establishing transportation and distribution infrastructure linking Asia and Europe

A consensus on peace and prosperity in Asia

capacity problem. However, there are also questions over how China can contribute to economic integration in Northeast Asia while it pursues such a goal.

The idea that the B&R Initiative will help resolve China's excess capacity problems is unconvincing. If the AIIB is very successful, then in five years it could lend US$ 20 billion per year — that is on a scale with the World Bank's International Bank for Reconstruction and Development lending. But just in steel alone, China would need US$ 60 billion per year of extra demand to absorb excess capacity. Figure 3.1 excludes excess capacity in cement, construction, and heavy machinery. The point is that the AIIB is much too small to make a dent in China's excess capacity problem.

However, the B&R Initiative is more than just the AIIB. It started with the idea that nearby countries in Central Asia could benefit from more transport infrastructure, some of which China could finance bilaterally.

However, the economies of Central Asia are not that large, so the potential for investment is limited. Overland transportation will remain expensive compared with shipments by sea. For that reason, China added the idea of a maritime road — that is, the expansion of infrastructure along the sea-going routes from the Chinese coast through Southeast Asia to the Indian Ocean and all the way to Europe. A vast amount of world trade already traverses along this route. This means there is a high probability that the Chinese approach to Asian economic integration will focus on the maritime road first.

Fortunately, the Economic Research Institute for ASEAN and East Asia has developed the "Comprehensive Asian Development Plan 2.0" (CADP) and analyzed production networks, industrial agglomeration, and innovation hubs. Research results indicate that if the CADP and the Maritime Silk Road Initiative are combined, there is a high possibility that Northeast Asia will be integrated more effectively and economically than either plan could do on its own. Considering that the B&R Initiative emphasizes policy coordination and strengthening connectivity through infrastructure building by neighboring countries, coordination and harmonization of the B&R Initiative and CADP will contribute greatly to Northeast Asia's economic integration. One important point here, however, is that such an initiative and plan should concentrate not only on building hard infrastructure, but should also provide more concrete plans to build soft infrastructure to facilitate economic integration through such means as trade liberalization.

3.7 Conclusion

The B&R Initiative seems appropriate for the present political and economic development of China in line with its thinking regarding international relations. But this strategy comes with several potential risks for the countries involved, including a harsh terrain, long distances to markets, high costs, slow customs clearance procedures, corruption, political instability, and terrorism, and challenges related to China's domestic problems, tensions with its neighbors, and rivalries with other great powers.[4] Nonetheless, it is

---

[4]I. I. Pop, *Strengths and Challenges of China's "One belt, One road" Initiative* (Centre for Geopolitics & Security in Realism Studies, London, 2016).

a worthwhile venture and the successful implementation of the B&R Initiative should be encouraged and welcomed in Northeast Asia. There is much to be done to achieve success.

First, it is important to recognize that the view that the B&R Initiative can be a major solution to China's excess capacity problems is largely misguided. The contributions that these initiatives together make to China's demand are likely to be too small to be macroeconomically meaningful. Thus, China should concentrate more on the possibilities of cooperation with neighboring countries to let them join the B&R Initiative and to invite investment from these countries. To this end, China should develop a refined strategy to attract them to projects.

China's initiatives in Asia also are seen in many quarters as a setback for the United States. The US government contributed to this narrative through its efforts to discourage allies from joining the new AIIB. In the end, major American allies, such as the UK, Australia, and Korea, did join the Chinese initiative, and Japan is seriously considering becoming a member. However, this is likely to be just a temporary diplomatic setback for the United States. Many major economies in Asia, such as Australia, Singapore, Malaysia, Korea, and Vietnam, want to be part of both the Chinese initiatives (the AIIB and the B&R Initiative) and US-led initiatives, be it the TPP or another. This is clearly the smart approach. For Vietnam, for instance, a turn to the AIIB could improve infrastructure, while using the TPP framework would allow Hanoi to integrate its economy with the vast and innovative US economy. I argue that these different efforts are in fact complementary. The kind of infrastructure financed through Chinese initiatives represents the "hardware" of trade and investment, necessary but not sufficient to deepen integration. The TPP or TPP type of frameworks, meanwhile, represent the "software" of integration, reducing trade barriers, opening up services for trade and investment, and tackling various regulatory barriers to trade. There is a risk that the competing initiatives of China and the United States will lead to regional blocs and a disintegration of trade, but it is more likely that Sino-American competition will lead to strengthened institutions and deeper integration throughout Asia–Pacific. Thus, it is more likely that the result will be cooperation.

The CADP can complement the B&R Initiative based on CADP's emphasis on soft infrastructure. However, we should also support a China–Japan–Korea Free Trade Agreement and the Regional Comprehensive

Economic Partnership, both of which can further strengthen economic cooperation and encourage better and more comprehensive soft infrastructure. With these supporting mechanisms, the B&R Initiative could have an even greater long-term impact on China's neighbors as well as the rest of the world. Although the infrastructure development will help China lessen some structural domestic GDP concerns, the B&R Initiative also has the potential to build stronger ties in the region and provide new leadership opportunities for Beijing. In the future, if regional tensions are wisely managed, this could lead to a more united Asia on international issues and strengthen the region's collective leverage and geopolitical power.

CHAPTER 4

The Belt and Road Initiative and Sustainable Development

Shirish Garud

*Energy-Environment Technology Development Division,
The Energy and Resources Institute (TERI), New Delhi, India*

We had interesting discussions and interesting points about the Belt and Road (B&R) Initiative. This chapter attempts to provide a slightly different perspective from the viewpoint of sustainable development agenda.

The B&R Initiative is being perceived as the Chinese initiative to create market and develop strategic alliance. However, this is an overall perception. The first is that the initiative needs huge investments and it is also associated with huge risks, both external and internal. Second, of course, we cannot forget that countries have their own development agendas and they are looking at these investments as part of their development strategy. And last, countries have agreed on Paris Climate Change agreement to achieve their declaration and Intended Nationally Determined Commitments toward Climate Change.

So, this chapter focuses on whether we can link the development agenda of the B&R Initiative with sustainable development agenda of the UN and Paris Climate Change agreement. This will not only help in these countries building infrastructures but building it in a sustainable way and providing access to modern energies for their citizens because many of these countries have large populations, which is not even connected to electricity.

Then countries can explore investments through Climate Change funds and BRICS Bank initiatives and other initiatives, which can support the Chinese investment. So, I think these two agendas can match with each other.

What UN says is sustainable energy for all empowered leaders to break partnerships and unlock finances to achieve universal access to sustainable energy as a contribution to a cleaner and prosperous world for all. This is what the global or larger agenda of the B&R Initiative is.

The major issues faced by these countries are sustainable development, access to energy, and climate-resilient infrastructure. Since we are talking of large investments across the globe in all 60 or so countries, infrastructure has to be climate-resilient because climate change impact is now visible and on the increase.

Looking at sustainable development agenda, the UN has come out with a number of sustainable development goals. We can look at three major ones. The 7th Goal is to ensure accessible, reliable, sustainable, and modern energy for all.

Energy is central to any development agenda. We cannot have development without energy. Globally, about 20% of the population still does not have access to electricity. Energy is also a key to climate change mitigation strategy, as more than 60% of GHG emissions, which is greenhouse gas emissions, which are responsible for climate change, are due to fossil energy use. When we are implementing new development, we should definitely look at sustainable and climate-responsive energy utilization.

Still about 2.5 billion people use polluting or inefficient cooking fuels such as wood. Majority of this population live in countries associated with the B&R Initiative. Again, the countries which are on the B&R Initiative face this development dilemma. As the majority of this population resides in these countries, the initiative can also take this into consideration. Human development index and energy use are often related, the countries which are high on the human development index are also using a high amount of energy. So, it is also important that if we are going ahead with development in these countries, it will also in turn increase their energy consumption and one should look at sustainable energy through renewable energy and energy efficiency initiatives.

Second, the 8th Goal is to promote inclusive and sustainable economic growth, full and productive employment and decent work for all. Unemployment has been increasing globally from 170 million in 2007 to nearly 202 million in 2012, out of which 75 million are young women and men. If we are not going to provide enough employment opportunities, then this may result in an unstable social fabric.

This agenda is also important and the B&R Initiative can not only generate employment for Chinese citizens but also globally or at least in countries where this initiative is being implemented.

So, we need around 470 million jobs globally for new people who are entering the labor market between now and 2030. There is a huge requirement for job creation and initiatives like the B&R Initiative can definitely look into this aspect.

Third, the 9th Goal is to build resilient infrastructure, promote inclusive and sustainable industrialization and foster innovation. Basic infrastructure is definitely required in many developing countries. Manufacturing can also be an important employer. Also, one can look at the infrastructure development which will promote sustainable industrialization.

Another important aspect is the risk of climate change for all countries. If you look at the B&R Initiative map, you find countries we are talking about are also prone to high climate change risk through floods, droughts, typhoons, etc. Recently, the world had just experienced one such event. This is also an important factor, especially when development is going to take place in infrastructure.

Climate change is a reality, and this is why the COP 21 last year and the Paris Agreement are important aspects. Countries have agreed to do something about mitigation and adaptation of climate change impacts through their INDCs, and it is expected that this agreement will come into force soon because all major countries have already signed the agreement. Of course, the agreement involves enhanced use of renewable energy, energy efficiency, and adaptive measures.

So, going forward, China may look to ensure the financing of infrastructure development based on strong policy frameworks in these countries which basically take into consideration the public opinion as mentioned earlier. Sustainable development principles could be at the core of this initiative of infrastructure trade and economic development.

It is important that industrial development happens on sustainable development principles and climate change adaptation and mitigation are part of this strategic development. Sound policies for climate-resilient infrastructure development are the need of the hour, and this initiative can help countries to adopt such policies if required. It is important to ensure that infrastructure investment is aligned with the Paris Agreement commitment of the involved nations, so that it will also help them meet their commitments.

Last but not the least, the B&R Initiative can serve as the goal of common destiny because we are also looking at threats coming from our actions to our destiny.

Part 2

The Belt and Road Initiative and Construction of "Hard Power"

CHAPTER 5

The Belt and Road Initiative and the Infrastructure Development in Laos

Lattana Thavonsouk

Institute of Foreign Affairs, Vientiane, Laos

After the Cold War, economic development has become the spearhead to propel the country. In doing so, development of the country's infrastructure is classified as the catalyst and the main factor conducive to the prosperity and well-being of people. The aftermath of the Cold War provides the opportunity for countries in the region to cluster with the aim to lessen the psychological barrier. Regional cooperation happens due to the globalization process that provides unlimited opportunities for countries in the region to sustain growth. It is obvious that the 21st century is an era of economic globalization and multipolarization of the world, a century of liberalization and development, and a century of peace, cooperation, openness, mutual learning, and resilience.

The quality of being a land-locked country with poor infrastructure has put a constraint on the socio-economic development of Laos, in addition to the legacy of war that still remains as a threat to the daily life of the peasants who are the backbones of the country. While many developing countries consider agriculture as the basic foundation to move forward and achieve progress and some countries even became the tigers of Asia, in the case of Laos, agricultural development moves very slow due to

45

some constraints. One of them is that the arable land is still covered by the unexploded ordnances. Many peasants met their destiny while working on their farm land saturated by bomblets which became obstacles to their routine tasks on the rice field.

Nevertheless, to get rid of this impediment, a "land-linked" strategy was introduced in parallel to regional and subregional infrastructure development trends, especially the frameworks of, among others, the ASEAN, Greater Mekong Sub-region, and Triangle Development Area. The strategy addresses the importance of infrastructure development, particularly the road/transport sector, as the means to achieve the 2020 vision for the country to graduate from the list of Less Developed Countries (LDCs) and to eradicate mass poverty in the country.

Economically, Laos still lags behind the rest of ASEAN countries in terms of economic development. This step will pose a big burden not only for ASEAN integration but also for the rest of the East Asian countries. This factor prevents the benefits of integration from being realized. If this large disparity cannot be solved, then the gap may widen and cause strong impact to the whole region, impeding the overall endeavor to achieve the regional integration as agreed earlier. As a result, the vicious circle will persist undoubtedly.

Due to the globalization era when the economic development becomes the catalyst for each country, Laos seizes this opportunity to exploit its central location in the Mekong subregion to foster much needed trade and investments. Strongly committed to integration in the regional and global system, Laos has its eyes on transforming itself from a land-locked country to a land-linked country through the economic corridors crossing its territory.

Infrastructure development has been identified as significant both in poverty reduction and private sector development. There are two reasons behind this: First, focusing on farm-to-market road construction with proper mechanism to link rural farmers to the growing demand within the country and the region is significant for poverty reduction. Second, improvement of infrastructure, particularly factory-to-port transportation, is critical in enhancing business performance, export development, and economic growth. Third, widening choices for logistic transportation in the longer term of the infrastructure development strategy of the country will greatly boost growth and assist in the poverty reduction program.

The poor infrastructure system, together with the absence of the necessary logistics and the non-unification of the transport system with neighboring countries, serves as a critical problem in the development of the private sector since it raises the cost of transportation, thereby reducing the price competitiveness of Lao export products. This directly impacts the overall development of the country.

Under regional and subregional cooperation schemes, the so-called "land-linked" strategy has become a priority to develop the domestic road system enabling to link to neighboring countries in order to gradually transform the obstacle situation to an opportunity for national development.

Infrastructure development is regarded as important, particularly the road sector is considered as a key in the country's development. The development of roads has contributed to the development of other sectors, including agriculture and commerce as it eased market access and improved transportation, freight and trans-shipment of goods in the country as well as with neighboring countries. To achieve poverty eradication through employment-generated industrialization, the infrastructure is recognized as instrumental to the success of the industrialization effort.

Infrastructure development, especially transportation and communication, has always been a priority sector for Laos as it has direct and indirect relations to many issues. The Lao Expenditure and Consumption Survey (LECS2) and Participatory Poverty Assessments (PPA), for example, found a high correlation between lack of road access and severe poverty. The very poor (17% of the population) live in areas where infrastructure is particularly scarce. On average, the very poor maybe found at least 15 km from the main road. During the rainy season, 70% among them have no road access. The rural poor have identified this as one of the main causes of their poverty.

Lack of access to all-weather roads or roads of any kind has also meant lack of access to schools, health facilities, and other basic services, such as electricity and potable water. Thus, poor infrastructure results in intergenerational poverty in as much as the poor people have limited opportunity and capacity to climb out of their poverty.

The initiative was raised by the Chinese President Xi Jinping in October 2013. The Silk Road Economic Belt and the 21st Century Maritime Silk Road Initiative had called for the integration of the region into a cohesive economic area by building infrastructure, increasing cultural exchanges, and widening trade. The Silk Road aims to facilitate exchanges of goods, know-how, thus promoting economic, cultural, and social progress, facilitating dialogue and integration of different civilizations. This initiative is not only a vision but also an action plan that will be implemented in nearly 60 countries along the Belt and Road (B&R) Initiative to achieve economic policy coordination and carry out broader and more in-depth regional cooperation of higher standards.

Regional integration is an unavoidable phase toward economic globalization. The B&R Initiative will contribute to greater connectivity and complementarity across the sub-regions and help the establishment and improvement of Asia's supply chain, industrial chain, thus bringing the regional cooperation to a new level.

These initiatives foresee the infrastructure development and systematic innovation, which are conducive to an improved business environment in Laos and the region as a whole, facilitating the unimpeded flow of production factors, thus improving their distribution and lowering or removing costs, and trade and investment barriers.

Regional development plans are grounded in the building of an extensive infrastructure that integrates all countries into a unique growth area. A network of transnational roads and rail routes that links transport systems, power grids, and markets across and beyond the region of Southeast Asia is meant to facilitate full participation of this region and global economy by enhancing their competitiveness as an economic bloc.

At the hub of the emerging web of roadways lies Laos with the hope of exploiting its central location in the sub-region to foster the much needed trade and investments. Laos is strongly committed to regional integration and global trade system by transforming its land-locked location through the corridors crossing its territory.

Three projects are figured out to support the facilitation of the infrastructure that links with neighboring countries. First, the North–South Corridor land route starting from South Kumming China passes through Northern Laos to Thailand via the fourth friendship bridge across the

Mekong River. Besides providing GMS countries with access to a huge intraregional market by connecting China to Southeast Asia, this North–South Corridor is expected to contribute to Laos' growth. Lao people living along the corridor can have access to markets, extension services, income, and employment opportunities, thus enhancing the development potential. More generally, road and other infrastructure projects revolutionize the lives of ethnic communities, enticing them to move down and abandon subsistence agriculture for market-based activities. The North–South Economic Corridor has also facilitated a boom in trade between China and the other GMS economies.

Second, the East–West Economic Corridor linking Danang of Vietnam, Savannakhet of Laos, Mukdahanh of Thailand and Myanmar is a flagship project for the Greater Mekong Sub-region Program. This project is highly relevant to development needs at the national and regional levels. It was appropriately designed to support economic centers and to complement poverty reduction. The project is economically efficient and can help improve access to markets, employment opportunities, and social services.

The North–South Economic Corridor and East–West Corridor will promote not only trade and investment but also tourism.

Third, the railway development project starts from Kunming of China–Laos–Thailand–Malaysia–Singapore. This ambitious project is considered as a megaproject. China's B&R Initiative infrastructure megaprojects are hence welcome for it will help fulfil the tasks of industrialization and modernization efforts. Laos considers its section of this megaproject as the key to its development and has flagged the construction project as a major priority in its nation's 8th Five Year Plan.

Once completed, these three projects can serve as the facilities' connectivity, which has been the priority of Laos to transform its status. These projects could improve the connectivity of the infrastructure construction plans and technical standard systems. They can push forward the construction of international trunk passageways and form the infrastructure network connecting the Southeast Asian region.

It is obvious that the third project has been designed in the B&R Initiative linking China and Laos and beyond corresponding to the infrastructure development Plan of Laos. These projects will take advantage of international routes connecting the core cities along the B&R Initiative by using key economic industrial parks as cooperation platforms. In other words, Laos will benefit from producing and exporting its commodities to the neighboring countries, generating incomes with the aim to eradicate poverty which has been encompassed in the National Growth and Poverty Eradication Strategy since early 2004.

The high-speed railway will bridge the gap for Lao people to have access to technological capabilities, human resources development, capital, and foreign direct investment. These factors can help benefit the regional integration to be realized. In addition to this, this project can supply the material entitlements, health, and education and similarly may propel the region to a high plane, accelerating the overall endeavor to achieve the regional integration as agreed earlier. As a result, the vicious circle will be terminated undoubtedly.

The construction of the friendship tunnel, a key cross-border project on China–Laos railway, was officially started in Yunnan on 22 June, 2016, marking a practical step in the build-up of the Sino-Lao international railway, which forms a part of the Pan-Asia Railway Network. The cross-border tunnel has a length of 9.8 km, with 7.2 km in China and 2.6 km in Laos. The tunnel will be finished in 56 months, and it is intended to be a signature of the time-tested friendship between China and Laos. The tunnel will pass through the stratum which is embedded with mud rocks and sandstones, and such rough geographical condition could make it hard to carry out works.

According to the construction plan of the high-speed rail line, 154 bridges, 76 tunnels, and 31 train stations will be built. The project costs US$ 7 billion which is very costly, but this debt burden is regarded as a short-term sacrifice that will benefit the country in the long run.

It is estimated that this speed railway can carry about 3.98 million passengers per year for domestic trips and 9.65 million passengers for domestic plus cross-border trips. Besides that, it is estimated that more than 2.59 tons of cargo will be shifted per year, the 427 km railway will link Vientiane, the capital city with the Chinese border, and will pass through the urban areas in several provinces.

In general, the Belt and the Road Initiative is an important foundation for it will deepen cooperation between China and ASEAN while the

ASEAN Economic Community is under way. This project will no doubt solve the differences in economic development, mitigating diversity in terms of growth, facilitating cross-border trade cooperation, making Southeast Asia a perfect market for China and vice versa and facilitating both sides to work together in the financial field. ASEAN is an important base for the China-proposed B&R Initiative, having it as a starting point, and the upcoming establishment of the ASEAN Community will benefit both the bloc and its partners including China.

The B&R Initiative has huge potential for ASEAN and China to cooperate in infrastructure construction and cross-border trade cooperation.

To support the B&R Initiative, China has set the Asian Infrastructure Investment Bank in October 2013 with the aim to lend the loans for the project of infrastructure. The AIIB, first proposed by China in October 2013, is a development bank dedicated to lending for projects regarding infrastructure. As of 2015, China announced that over one trillion yuan (US$ 160 billion) of infrastructure projects were in planning or construction.

To witness the construction of the high-speed railway, Laos and China had broken ground in Vientiane to start the construction of a high-speed rail megaproject to connect between China and Laos. This rail line will link China's Kunming all the way down to Singapore, passing through Laos, Thailand, Malaysia, and Singapore as the final destination of about 3,000 km.

Laos fully supports the building of a railway in a bid to free itself from the constraints of being land-locked, hoping to create a land link and become a transit hub with the region. The railway will lower transport costs and is expected to benefit the economy by attracting more foreign investment and providing much improved logistics services, boosting the socio-economic development of Laos, improving the nation's transportation and generating a lot of jobs for local people. Of course, it will also inject new momentum into the economy of China's southwestern regions. The national strategy will be upgraded to change its geographical disadvantages due to the megaproject initiatives.

The rail line shall enable interconnectivity once it is operational. It will give a significant boost to socio-economic development of Laos given that the current time-consuming high-cost road transport is among the core issues that discourage foreign investors in operating business in

Laos. Once completed, the farm goods from Laos will reach China within 2–3 h.

Three projects mentioned earlier would be of use in terms of contribution to the connectivity and eventual East Asian Community building regardless of the financial burden, which will be left for the generations to come.

The development of the infrastructure becomes a vital factor for the East Asian Community building for it can help sustain growth, easing the free flow of capital, people, and investment. ASEAN, the sole and viable organization in Southeast Asia, has been engaged in the cooperation with China, its giant neighbor, with the hope of bringing the B&R Initiative into a high plane. Around 20 years had elapsed, ASEAN–China dialogue relations have been developed constantly and effectively. China has shown its support for ASEAN's role as the driving force in the regional process. Clearly, ASEAN and China have been engaged in series of agreements for them to commit to obligations to bolster bilateral interaction.

Laos and China are good neighboring countries, sharing the border of 550 km, closely linked by common mountains and rivers, and have been keeping a profound traditional friendship since ancient times. Satisfied with the achievements in trade and economic cooperation, Laos and China attach great importance to deepen Laos–China economic and trade cooperation.

With the target to set the goal of developing bilateral ties of all-round cooperation characterized by long-term stability, good-neighborliness, friendship, and mutual trust, Laos and China signed many agreements and MOU including trade, investment protection, and tourism. The committee on bilateral economic, trade, and technological cooperation was set up. This, in turn, will contribute to the services of the railway link between Kunming and Singapore in the future and facilitate the economic North–South Corridors (China–Laos–Thailand) by having Laos as a land-linked country. In this particular project, China shared half the cost of construction of the bridge across the Mekong River.

China ranks as the first investor, amounting over US$ 5 billion invested in Laos in 165 projects. According to the statistics from the Lao Ministry of Commerce and Industry, the Chinese investment concentrates on agriculture, fishery, food processing, construction, mining, and exploration. It is worth noting that the trade relations between Laos and China have achieved a great deal of progress. This is poised to increase with the involvement of the construction of the high-speed rail.

As neighbors, the economic and trade cooperation between eight northern provinces of Laos and Yunnan province is very encouraging. The cooperation in the field of communication is one of the important factors to promote economic and trade interaction. The two sides attach great importance to the improvement of the navigation along the Mekong River, with which the exchanges of goods will be increased in numbers.

CHAPTER 6

Russia–China Cooperation as a Part of the Belt and Road Initiative

K. A. Kokarev

Russian Institute for Strategic Studies, Moskva, Russia

The current international relations have a number of features which significantly influence the present situation in different parts all over the world. Among these features could be noted political instability in some countries and regions, the difficulties of recovering process of economies and financial stability in many countries after the global crisis of 2008, the consecutive increase of non-traditional threats, and attempts of the USA and some of its allies to preserve western domination in the international political and economic system.

China's initiative the Silk Road Economic Belt and the 21st century Maritime Silk Road (the Belt and Road) is of particular importance not only for China but also for the countries interested in maintaining stability and mutually beneficial cooperation in such unfavorable external conditions.

As you know, in March 2015 the document "Vision and Actions on Jointly Building Silk Road Economic Belt and 21st Century Maritime Silk Road" was published in China. In essence, it is a "roadmap" for the Belt and Road (B&R) Initiative proposed by President Xi Jinping in 2013. We believe, the initiative has been in line with constructive trend in regional and global development. From the point of view of China's neighbors, the initiative is in the interest of countries seeking to strengthen their economic power through participation in this transcontinental project.

China emphasizes that the initiative is not heading to undermine or eliminate the current economic system and institutions. It represents a desire for a peaceful and mutually beneficial exchange. The existing world order is viewed in Beijing as a major cornerstone of global stability. Nevertheless, according to the opinion of Chinese experts, this world order needs to be improved, and more opportunities for developing countries should be opened. Therefore, the Chinese initiative is aimed at preservation and development of free trade and equal cooperation, which make it possible for all interested countries to profitably participate in realizing the B&R Initiative. We believe, the Chinese initiative's impact on the regional and global development is likely to be very strong, because the countries along the Silk Road Economic Belt are home to more than 60% of the world population, and today they have been producing about 30% of the global GDP.

An international significance of the initiative is also determined by the fact that it might effectively promote the UN program of "sustainable development of the world for the period up to 2030." In particular, large-scale infrastructure investments and other projects highlighted by China could mitigate global poverty, increase agricultural production, improve food security, etc.

To promote its projects outside of China, Beijing strives to cooperate closely with its partners through establishing effective win–win relations. It reflects their mutual desire to create favorable opportunities for growth through a simultaneous implementation of both China's partners' strategic plans and China's Silk Road Economic Belt. Instances of this policy toward neighboring countries and other states can be seen in China's cooperation with Russia, Kazakhstan, Mongolia, Korea, the European Union, etc.

Russia has always been a supporter of establishing closer economic cooperation between different countries situated in Asia and Europe. In 2010, Vladimir Putin had suggested a creative idea to establish an economic community of different nations and promote advanced economic integration on the territory from Lisbon to Vladivostok. It should also be noted that some practical steps have been taken in this direction, namely, the Customs Union was created in 2010, the Common Economic Space was established in 2012, and the Eurasian Economic Union has began to function in the year 2015.

At present, Russia and China have been moving to a new quality of bilateral relations. Improving their trade-economic and cultural links, they also intensify regular consultations on important issues of international development, including problems pertinent to the structure of emerging world order. Therefore, it was quite a natural decision to sign a Joint Declaration on cooperation in coordinating development of the Eurasian Economic Union and the Silk Road Economic Belt. The document focuses not only on the development of trade-economic links, mutually beneficial industrial and scientific cooperation, bilateral investment, and financial bonds, but it also aims at updating international transport-logistics infrastructure and consecutively creating necessary conditions to build a free trade area between the members of the Eurasian Economic Union and the People's Republic of China.

A major goal of the cooperation within the framework of the two projects is to create a favorable environment for thorough development of the countries participating in the projects. In particular, the cooperation in compliance with the document should contribute to growth in Russian–Chinese trade which is likely to increase to US$ 200 billion by 2020, as was officially declared by the two leaders — Russia's President V. Putin and the President of the People's Republic of China Xi Jinping. We also hope that the conjugation in building of the Eurasian Economic Union and the Silk Road Economic Belt will make it possible to elevate the efficiency of Eurasian transport network to a new level. We believe, it is also a real opportunity to turn Russia's Siberia and the Far east into a bridge between Europe and East Asia. Unfortunately, at present Russia's highways and railways account for only 5–7% of the Eurasian transport and logistics market.

Of course, the infrastructure building provides participating countries with the opportunity to use the projects in the interest of their own development. However, it will not guarantee success. In this case, it would be better for the countries to have their own strategies of participation in the B&R Initiative. It means, before entering into the projects, it is necessary for the country to set appropriate financial and economic strategy as well other conditions that will allow making the two projects beneficial to the maximum.

Having declared a close bilateral interaction, Russia and China have offered genuine creative projects. These projects have been aimed not only at consolidating efforts to implement broad economic programs (trade, manufacturing and investment sectors, transport and logistics infrastructure), but also strengthening the other relations, including in the humanitarian sector. We believe, upholding equal rights and agreements is a reliable way to develop mutual trust and durable peace and stability. Such principles will also promote successful solutions of engendering problems in the relations between the partners.

The signing of the above-mentioned Joint Declaration is an adequate Russian response to China's initiative to build the Silk Road Economic Belt. Moreover, according to Russia's President V. Putin, Moscow and Beijing have begun negotiations on establishing a "comprehensive trade and economic partnership with the member-states of the Eurasian Economic Union (EEU), the Commonwealth of Independent States, India, Pakistan and perhaps Iran in future.

We believe that a closer cooperation between EEU and the European Union should also be involved in joint development of the EEU and the Silk Road Economic Belt. Such collaboration is likely to contribute to more effective implementation of many projects of both the EEU and the Silk Road Economic Belt. Therefore, Russia and China should cooperate more closely and be more active in the triangle: Russia–China–EU.

In our opinion, close cooperation between the countries in the framework of the EEU and the Silk Road Economic Belt might create a wide international platform that could become an asymmetrical response to the West's attempts to hinder changes for improving the global system of political and economic relations in the 21st century.

CHAPTER 7

Central Asia and the Silk Road Economic Belt

Kemel Toktomushev

Institute of Public Policy and Administration,
University of Central Asia, Tajikistan, Kyrgyz Republic

7.1 Introduction

In the early 2000s, Chinese-Central Asian trade was estimated around US$ 1billion; in 2010–2013, these numbers reached nearly US$ 50 billion.[1] In a decade, China grew from providing a limited number of imports to Central Asia to providing more than 10% of the region's total imports, while simultaneously becoming one of the main export destinations for Central Asian goods and commodities.[2] It is estimated that the real numbers are even more staggering due to the significant volume of informal imports and exports.

Aside from being a key trading partner, China became the region's largest *de facto* lender and source of development financing. For example,

---

[1] C. Putz, Will all roads in Central Asia eventually lead to China? *The Diplomat*, 9 June 2015, Available at http://thediplomat.com/2015/06/will-all-roads-incentral-asia-eventually-lead-to-china/ (accessed on 27 April 2016).

[2] R. Mogilevskii, Trends and patterns in foreign trade of Central Asian Countries, Institute of Public Policy and Administration Working Paper No. 1, Bishkek (2012).

China has already financed several multimillion-dollar projects in Kyrgyzstan, including the construction of the Datka electricity substation and the 405 km Datka–Kemin transmission line. China also agreed to a US$ 400 million loan to construct Kyrgyzstan's North–South alternative road. As of 2015, Kyrgyzstan owed China approximately US$ 1.8 billion, which comprises nearly half of Kyrgyzstan's total external debt. In a similar vein, the government-sponsored Export-Import Bank of China remains Tajikistan's largest single creditor, holding almost 46% of Tajikistan's total external debt.[3] Furthermore, China is well situated to act as a mediator in Central Asia: The China–Central Asia pipeline consists of three separate enterprises, each based on a 50% ownership agreement between China and Kazakhstan, China and Uzbekistan, and China and Turkmenistan (see Footnote 1). Moreover, through its China National Petroleum Corporation (CNPC), China is continuing to invest significantly in the region's transport and energy infrastructure, including the construction of the Atyrau–Alashankou crude oil pipeline.

Accordingly, Central Asian leadership must revisit its approach toward China and utilize the opportunities such a neighborhood offers in a more constructive and mutually beneficial way. Central Asian policies toward China should be pragmatic and forward looking. In this regard, the Chinese-led Belt and Road (B&R) Initiative offers an excellent opportunity for the region's leadership to practice evidence-based decision-making and capitalize on China's willingness to advance regional integration for the benefit of the broader population.

The Silk Road Economic Belt and Maritime Silk Road, also known as the B&R Initiative, is a Chinese-led development framework that aims to integrate trade and investment in Eurasia. Presented by the Chinese President Xi Jinping during his official visits to Kazakhstan and Indonesia in 2013, the B&R Initiative is an ambitious initiative aimed at reviving the historic Silk Road in the 21st century by connecting China with Europe via Central Asia, South Asia, Southeast Asia, West Asia, East Africa, and the Middle East. Based on implementation guidelines released by China's National Development and Reform Commission (2015), the B&R

---

[3] World Bank Group, Tajikistan. A moderate slowdown in economic growth coupled with a sharp decline in household purchasing power, Tajikistan Economic Update, no. 2 (2015).

Initiative seeks to promote policy coordination, facilities connectivity, unimpeded trade, financial integration, and "people-to-people bond."

The proposed land-based Silk Road Economic Belt constitutes an infrastructure network of roads, rail and oil and gas pipelines stretched across the Eurasian continent. The Maritime Silk Road would be its proposed maritime equivalent, establishing an economic corridor through a system of linked ports and infrastructure. Once fully completed, the B&R Initiative is projected to directly affect nearly 4.4 billion people with a collective GDP of US$ 21 trillion[4]; Central Asia is assigned a special role in this regional architecture. President Xi Jinping visited every Central Asian state to personally reassure the local leadership of the Chinese commitment by investing US$ 40 billion in the region's infrastructure through the Silk Road Infrastructure Fund. The recent unveiling of the China-backed US$ 100 billion Asian Infrastructure Investment Bank (AIIB) confirms Beijing's determination to advance its vision of regional integration. The Economist reports that China plans to spend a total of US$ 1 trillion in government funds through AIIB and the China Development Bank on the B&R Initiative. Moreover, in the summer of 2015, the credit rating agency Moody's produced a report rating the B&R Initiative as credit positive for the emerging market countries involved. Specifically, Moody's predicts that the Chinese-led initiatives will mostly benefit smaller countries with underdeveloped infrastructure, low per-capita incomes, and low investment rates, as President of China Xi Jinping expects trade via the modern Silk Road to surpass US$ 2.5 trillion in a decade.

Accordingly, in Sections 7.2 and 7.3, policy recommendations are suggested for both the governments of Central Asian states and the Chinese government with the aim of capitalizing on China's role in the region through more pragmatic and mutually beneficial engagement.

7.2 Policy Recommendations for Central Asian Governments

Policy recommendations for the governments of Central Asia are as follows:

- Central Asian leadership must recognize the *de facto* role of China as the main economic and development player in the region and

---

[4]BDO, *The Belt and Road* (BDO Advisory Pte Ltd, Singapore, 2015).

develop their countries' respective policies from an evidence-based perspective;

- Central Asian state leaders should address the growing Sinophobia in the region and mitigate its repercussions;
- Central Asian leadership must utilize the opportunities to improve infrastructure and stimulate economic growth offered by the Silk Road Economic Belt; and
- Central Asian leadership has to recognize that the Silk Road Economic Belt is more than an infrastructure project. This initiative assumes the fortification of "people-to people-bond", involving cultural and academic exchanges, joint research, forums and fairs, personnel trainings, and exchanges and visits under the framework of existing bilateral and multilateral cooperation mechanisms. Accordingly, all possible opportunities should be explored.

7.3 Policy Recommendations for the Chinese Government

Chinese leadership should seek constructive engagement with other actors in the region, particularly Russia.

Russia and China already work together in Central Asia under the auspices of the Shanghai Cooperation Organization (SCO), and Central Asia is the natural region to observe greater cooperation between Moscow and Beijing. The SCO was established initially in 1996 as the Shanghai Five to set the framework for strategic cooperation on matters related to security on border regions between Kazakhstan, Kyrgyzstan, Tajikistan, Russia, and China. In 2001, the goals of the organization were reformulated to include political, economic, and military cooperation. The birth of the SCO was immediately regarded by many analysts and policymakers as a potential balancing tool of Russia and China to counter the growing American engagement in Central Asia.

Yet, to date, such a view has not been materialized. Certainly, in the span of the last 20 years, the SCO did achieve some remarkable milestones. The leaders of the SCO member-states managed to attenuate historical border tensions, establish procedural mechanisms of cooperation, and advance common discourses on the evils of terrorism, separatism, and extremism. Notwithstanding such developments, the SCO failed to project the image of an effective regional organization and has been perceived more so as a discussion forum to promote confidence and good-neighbor relations among member-states. Beijing remained reluctant to get engaged directly in the security matters of Central Asia through SCO, notwithstanding its concerns with Islamic separatism in Xinjiang. In a similar vein, Moscow resisted the Chinese initiatives to turn the SCO into a more development and economic-based platform.

In this respect, a Sino-Russian rapprochement may animate the SCO. In fact, Beijing may become the powerhouse of the SCO by guiding the organization in a new direction. The enhanced cooperation between Russia and China may also foster new bilateral and multilateral initiatives and have a positive impact on the region. For example, in addition to the development of a Eurasian economic corridor, China and Russia may coordinate efforts to jointly address emerging threats in Central Asia, such as drug and human trafficking and the rise of radical Islamism.

Chinese leadership should pragmatically assess both the internal and external constraints facing the Silk Road Economic Belt project's successful implementation in Eurasia in general and in Central Asia in particular, before disbursing a vast amount of resources toward the creation of a substantial infrastructure network.

CHAPTER 8

Inward FDI Determinants and FDI Influence on Economic Growth in the Kyrgyz Republic: An Empirical Analysis

**Almazbek Mukarapov, Nargiza Alymkulova
and Gulasel Shamshieva**

*Finance and Banking Department, International Ataturk
Alatoo University, Bishkek, Kyrgyzstan*

8.1 Introduction

Foreign direct investment (FDI) is crucial for the developing countries and countries with transition economies as these countries are on the way to achieve a sustainable economic growth. Today, in the economy of the Kyrgyz Republic, one of the accelerating factors in the transformation of the national economy is attraction and effective use of FDI. This chapter examines the determinants of inward FDI in the Kyrgyz Republic first and the effect of FDI on economic growth further by employing multiple linear regression model by using time-series data from 1993 to 2014. According to the study results, the most significant determinants of inward FDI are GDP, GNI, inflation, exchange rate, technicians as a percent of total R&D personnel. There is a very strong positive correlation between FDI and GDP, and this relationship is statistically significant for the Kyrgyz Republic. The presented empirical study results have a crucial role for policymakers of the transition economy of the Kyrgyz Republic to undertake the utmost and valid macroeconomic policy in the country to attract FDI.

FDI is a key element in international economic integration. FDI creates direct, stable, and long-lasting links between economies. It encourages the transfer of technology and know-how between countries, and allows the host economy to promote its products more widely in international markets. FDI is both the consequence of and a contributing factor toward making the international economic system open and more effective.[1] FDI is also an additional source of funding for investment and, under the right policy environment, it can be an important vehicle for development. While international trade has doubled, flows of FDI have increased by a factor of 10 around the world.[2]

In theory, FDI seems to yield more benefits than other types of financial flows since, in addition to augmenting domestic capital stock, it has a positive impact on productivity growth through transfers of technology and managerial expertise.[3]

According to Stiglitz, "the argument for FDI is compelling. Such investment brings with it not only resources, but technology, access to markets, and (hopefully) valuable training, an improvement in human capital. FDI is also not as volatile — and therefore as disruptive — as the short-term flows."[4]

Instruments of public and private foreign investment (FDI) and external trade are central to the process of long-term economic development,

---

[1] J. Sohinger and W. G. Harrison, The implications of foreign direct investment for development in transition countries: challenges for the Croatian economy, *Eastern European Economics*, **42** (1) (2004) 56–74.

[2] E. Yeyati, U. Panizza and E. Stein, The cyclical nature of north-south FDI flows. *Journal of International Money and Finance*, **26** (2007) 104–130.

[3] L. De Mello, Foreign direct investment in developing countries and growth: A selective survey, *The Journal of Development Studies*, **34** (1) (1997) 1–34.

[4] J. J. Stiglitz, Capital market liberalization, economic growth, and instability, *World Development*, **28** (2000) 1075–1086.

especially for developing and transition economies across the world.[5] It has often been argued that FDI inflow is one of the driving forces of economic growth in developing countries.[6]

However, developing countries are generally unable to exploit the benefits from their abundant natural resources due to inadequate human and physical capital and technological know-how.[7]

In fact, up to the year 2007, the year in which a record global FDI inflow of US$ 1.9 trillion was reached, transition countries were the second most important destination market for FDI, the first being emerging Asia.[8] In this sense, FDI may also become sustainable growth factors through their specific benefits on the national economy, through their positive spillovers associated to vertical foreign investments and intra-industry specialization.[9] Lesser-Developed Countries (LDCs) have an incentive to strengthen areas and aspects of their economy or government that are heavily scrutinized by firms that are considering a possible long-term investment.[10] Foreign firms may have efficiency and other "spillover" effects on local competitors (horizontal spillovers) as well as on upstream and downstream domestic firms (vertical spillovers).[11]

---

[5] UNCTAD (United Nations Conference on Trade and Development) Book review World Investment Report 2006, FDI from Developing and Transition Economies: Implications for Development, *Journal of Asian Economics*, **18** (2007) 553–561 (United Nations, New York).

[6] J. S. Mah, Foreign direct investment in flows and economic growth of China, *Journal of Policy Modeling*, **32** (2010) 155–158.

[7] S. Iamsiraroj and M. A. Ulubasoglu, Foreign direct investment and economic growth: A real relationship or wishful thinking?, *Economic Modelling*, **51** (2015) 200–213.

[8] J. Hanousek, Evžen Kočenda and M. Maurel, Direct and indirect effects of FDI in emerging European markets: A survey and meta-analysis, *Economic Systems*, **35** (2011) 301–322.

[9] Z. Gheorghe and V. Vasile, Macroeconomic impact of FDI in Romania, Emerging markets queries in finance and business, *Procedia Economics and Finance*, **3** (2012) 3–11.

[10] J. Lewis, Factors influencing foreign direct investment in lesser developed countries, *The Park Place Economist*, **VIII** (2000) 99–107.

[11] Y. Gorodnichenko, J. Svejnar and K. Terrell, When does FDI have positive spillovers? Evidence from 17 transition market economies, *Journal of Comparative Economics*, **42** (2014) 954–969.

Therefore, the aim of this chapter is to investigate the determinants of FDI in the Kyrgyz Republic. Nonetheless, the effect of the FDI on economic growth of the republic is also studied.

8.2 Theoretical Framework of FDI

In order to be able to compete in a foreign market, an investing company must have some ownership-specific assets in technology knowledge, management, marketing, organization, etc. The macro-level eclectic theories of FDI view international production through a simultaneous presence of the three types of advantages, or the OLI (ownership, location, and internalization) paradigm. Nevertheless, the OLI paradigm has remained the dominant analytical framework for accommodating a variety of operationally testable economic theories of the determinants of FDI.[12] Notwithstanding, the literature on FDI identifies the three most common investment motivations: market-seeking, asset-seeking or resource-seeking, efficiency-seeking.[13]

The first type of FDI is called market-seeking FDI, where investor's purpose is to serve local markets. It is also referred to as horizontal FDI because investor replicates the production facilities in host country. The reason for horizontal FDI is market size and the market growth.

The second type of FDI is asset-seeking or resource-seeking FDI. It takes place when the company's purpose is to gain access or acquire the resources in the host country, which are not available in home country, such as raw materials, natural resources, or low-cost labor.

The third type of FDI is efficiency-seeking FDI. It takes place when the company can gain while there is a common governance of geographically dispersed activities and presence of economies of scope and scale.

If we sum up all the three different types of FDI, then the attracting factors of the above-described FDIs are low-labor cost, large domestic

---

[12] J. H. Dunning, The eclectic paradigm as an envelope for economic and business theories of MNE activity, *International Business Review*, **9** (2000) 163–190.

[13] A. Kudina and M. Jakubiak, The motives and impediments to FDI in the CIS, *Global Forum VII on International Investment*, 8 April 2008, p. 32.

market, richness in natural resources, and close proximity to developed western countries. The countries with favorable condition in those factors would attract more FDI.

The most widespread is the classification proposed by the experts in UNCTAD.[14] In this report, experts identify three main groups of such factors:

(1) The general policy of the country in relation to FDI, including political and social stability; rules governing access and operations of foreign companies; the mode of activity of foreign affiliates of the companies; the policy regarding the functioning and structure of markets (especially policy toward competition and regulation of mergers and acquisitions); international agreements that regulate FDI; privatization policy; trade policy (tariffs and non-tariff barriers) and coherence of trade policy with the policy on FDI; tax policy.

(2) Measures of facilitation of doing business, including promotion of investments (including the establishment of the country's image in the eyes of potential investors, support of foreign investors in all stages of investment project implementation, as well as services to facilitate business); benefits and other incentives for foreign investors, eliminating the "by-costs related to corruption, ineffective administrative management, etc.; social development with the purpose of adaptation and attraction to the staff abroad for the implementation of the investment project.

(3) Economic factors, including market size and growth; market structure; revenues per capita (reflect purchasing power within the country); access to regional and global markets; consumer preferences, specific for country; the availability of raw materials and resources; cost and workforce skills, technological innovations and other created assets (trademarks, brands); infrastructure (ports, roads, telecommunications, etc.); the cost of existing resources and assets productivity of labor; other operating costs (costs of transport

---

[14]UNCTAD, *World Investment Report 2014: Investing in SDGs: An Action Plan* (2014).

and communication, intermediate materials); participation in regional integration groupings, contributing to the establishment of regional corporate networks.

In general, the first two groups of factors selected by the experts of UNCTAD, affecting the inflow of FDI, can be described as institutional factors, i.e., factors related to the regulation of economic processes, political, and legal environment.

FDI contributes to the emergence of new high-technological industries, modernization of fixed assets, creation of additional workplaces, active usage of qualified human resources, introduction of advanced achievements in the field of management, marketing, saturation of the domestic market with high-quality goods and increase of export. Such investments, compared with foreign loans, do not increase the debts of the country, thereby reducing the outflow of currency abroad. They do not burden the national budget and allow one to direct significant financial resources in the key sectors of the economy.

Prominent western economists S. Smith, G. Haberer, G. Mayer, and others repeatedly emphasize in their works that planning for economic growth in developing countries is unthinkable in modern conditions without the possibility of access for foreign capital in the economy of the country. They note that the impact of foreign capital in developing countries will have a positive effect in all respects regardless of the form in which it invades into the national economy, in the form of private direct investment or loans from international financial institutions.

Private direct investment in the industry from their claim not only brings a measurable increase of national wealth to developing countries but also entails the inflow of foreign professionals who contribute to raising the technical and cultural levels of the country, facilitating the training of skilled personnel and introduction of the most modern technology and management methods.

The need for FDI is increasing since the majority of enterprises are in debt, growing overdue debt, reducing public investment in industry, aging fixed assets. The industry needs new equipment and progressive technologies. Most businesses face the problem of closure and organization in their place with new truly modern production. Thus, the import of international capital in Kyrgyzstan today is one of the most effective and speedy ways to revive the Kyrgyzstan economy.

8.3 Inward FDI in the Kyrgyz Republic

Today, in the economy of the Kyrgyz Republic, one of the accelerating factors in the transformation of the national economy is attraction and effective and efficient exploitation of FDI. All these are possible with a favorable investment climate.

In attracting FDI, the growing competition will certainly contribute to the development of economy and stimulate reforms aimed at improving investment climate and attracting major foreign investments. The availability of strategically important resources, the high level of population literacy rate, the cheapness of skilled labor, comparative infrastructure and social services, the proximity to the Eurasian market, undoubtedly, benefit the transition economies in attracting FDI. However, experience has shown that these factors are not enough, and the comprehensive structural reforms and active state support are necessary.

In the economy of the Kyrgyz Republic, the FDI inflow might serve a very crucial role and have an impact on economic growth of the country. The message of the President of the Kyrgyz Republic "Social development of people in Kyrgyzstan — a solid economic foundation" on 30 September 1998 set the goal of achieving the level of growth of direct foreign investments up to 15% of GDP annually.

As shown in Figure 8.1, the inward FDI, as well as economic growth of the country, are not steadily growing rather rising up and falling down. From the independence of the Kyrgyz Republic, the average level of FDI to GDP could reach only 4.61%.[15] If we compare with other transition economies such as Montenegro, where the level is 22.07%, this might present us the picture of the current situation of FDI in the country.

The FDI flow on economic activities (see Table 8.1) demonstrates that the main shares of FDI go to manufacturing (37%), professional,

---

[15]N. B. Alymkulova and D. A. Musaeva, Foreign direct investment as a transmission channel of Great Recession (case of the Kyrgyz Republic), *Alatoo Academic Studies*, **3** (2015) 93–102.

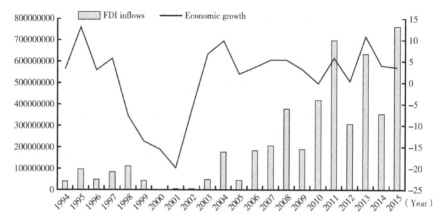

Figure 8.1: FDI to GDP in the Kyrgyz Republic.

Source: World Bank Indicators (http://data.worldbank.org/).

Table 8.1: The Flow of FDI on Economic Activities During the Period of 2008–2014.

Items	2008	2009	2010	2011	2012	2013	2014
Mining and quarrying	0.87	0.96	0.15	3.12	4.35	2.40	10.31
Manufacturing	27.41	23.23	49.75	57.65	43.55	32.94	37.31
Electricity, gas, steam and air conditioning supply	0.00	0.00	0.00	0.00	0.00	1.68	5.99
Water supply; sewerage, waste management and remediation activities	0.15	0.05	0.00	0.00	0.01	0.02	0.00
Construction	5.65	3.24	1.94	0.75	4.71	1.61	2.76
Wholesale and retail trade; repair of motor vehicles and motorcycles	6.49	8.01	8.03	7.65	5.52	6.90	5.17
Transportation and storage	1.75	1.33	1.83	4.31	1.09	1.04	0.83
Financial and insurance activities	40.08	37.85	5.24	5.67	7.15	10.35	3.92
Professional, scientific and technical activities	16.94	22.39	31.64	19.96	31.63	41.82	31.44
Accommodation and food service activities	0.28	0.72	1.22	0.47	0.30	0.05	0.03
Other	0.38	2.22	0.2	0.42	1.69	1.19	2.24
Total	100	100	100	100	100	100	100

Source: Database of the National Statistics Committee of the Kyrgyz Republic (www.stat.kg).

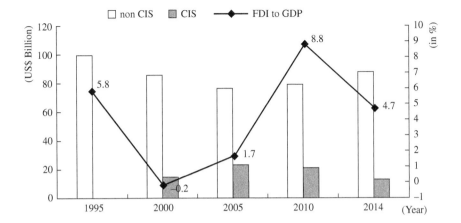

Figure 8.2:   FDI Inwards in the Kyrgyz Republic.
Source: World Bank Indicators (http://data.worldbank.org/).

scientific, and technical activities (31.44%). There is an inverse tendency between FDI flow to economic activities. Likewise, FDI flow to manufacturing has been increased by 10% and that to professional, scientific, and technical activities increased by 14.5% from 2008 to 2014, whereas flow to financial and insurance activities shrinked by 36.16% during the same period.

A large and continuously growing stock of FDI observed in transition economies include likewise approximately 70–85% of FDI from the following OECD countries: Austria, Belgium (and Luxembourg), Denmark, France, Germany, Italy, Japan, Korea, Netherlands, Portugal, Spain, UK, and US.[16] Consecutively, the structure of inward FDI in different countries is characterized by a capital investment of the CIS and non-CIS countries in the Kyrgyz Republic (see Figure 8.2). In this sense, inward FDI of the republic accounted for 100% from non-CIS countries. By contrast, this share declined from year to year through plumbing by 22%, which belongs to the inward FDI from CIS countries. Remarkably, FDI from non-CIS countries started to increase in 2014. On the other hand, the

---

[16]G. Cazzavillan and K. Olszewski, Interaction between foreign financial services and foreign direct investment in Transition Economies: An empirical analysis with focus on the manufacturing sector, *Research in Economics*, **66** (2012) 305–319.

FDI to GDP rate reached up to 5.8% in 1995, −0.2% in 2000, 1.7% in 2005, and 4.7% in 2014. The reason for such a kind of volatility may be described by divergent factors. This is what should be studied solely.

The volume and structure of FDIs in the Kyrgyz economy are greatly facilitated by the reflection of the investment climate, which, in the opinion of foreign investors, was not satisfactory. This situation mostly might be connected with the instability of domestic political and economic situation, such as deteriorating economic situation, shortcomings in economic legislation, and low professionalism of the management of economic structures to investment cooperation.

However, in any country, the overall growth of the economy is determined by the investments. Nevertheless, we see that, despite difficulties, attracting domestic and foreign investments in the economy yields positive results on economic growth.

8.4 Literature Review

8.4.1 *FDI Determinant Approach Literature*

With the integration of post-communist countries into the global economy after 1990, there has been a strong research interest in the role of FDI and multinational enterprises (MNEs) in economic restructuring and technological catch-up.[17]

An extensive body of literature focuses on the determinants of FDI on regional as well as separate country levels.

Nay Bevan and Estrin by using panel dataset studied the determinants of FDI into European transition economies within the period of 1994–2000. The authors followed the models of Helpman[18] and Brainard,[19] and employed the following factors: GDP, unit labor costs in

---

[17]A. Giroud, B. Jindra and P. Marek, Heterogeneous FDI in transition economies — A novel approach to assess the developmental impact of backward linkages, *World Development*, **40** (11) (2012) 2206–2220.

[18]E. Helpman, A simple theory of international trade with multinational corporation, *Journal of Political Economy*, **92** (1984) 451–471.

[19]S. L. Brainard, An empirical assessment of the proximity-concentration trade-off between multinational sales and trade, *American Economic Review*, **87** (1997) 520–544.

the host country, interest rate, openness to trade, and institutional, legal, and political risks.[20]

Bilgili *et al.* found the basic FDI determinants of Turkey through Markov regime-switching models.[21] The growth rates of FDI, GDP, alternative energy prices, export and import, indexes of labor cost in Turkey, country risks (confidence levels) in Turkey, US and EU, and discount rate in Turkey were analyzed in this study within the data from 1988 to 2010.

Hence, Lien and Filatotchev emphasized that a firm's decision to undertake FDI in the less-explored, riskier areas of an emerging economy is positively associated with the presence of large block shareholders.[22]

Savoiu and Taicu included FDI models based on a country risk, taking into account the fact that it plays a crucial role in FDI attractiveness.[23] Furthermore, Iloie analyzed the relation between FDI, corruption perception index, and country risk assessments for Central and Eastern Europe.

Holland and Pain investigated the FDI determinants for Eastern European transition economies as follows: the role of privatization, the external orientation of the host economies, labor costs and risks.[24]

Cevis and Camurdan estimated the economic determinants for 17 developing countries and transition economies by employing the model with seven explanatory economic variables: the previous period FDI, GDP growth, wage (unit labor costs), the trade openness of countries, the

---

[20]A. A. Bevan and S. Estrin, The determinants of foreign direct investment into European transition economies, *Journal of Comparative Economics*, **32** (2004) 775–787.

[21]F. Bilgili, N. S. Halici Tuluce and I. Dogan, The determinants of FDI in Turkey: A Markov regime-switching approach, *Economic Modelling*, **29** (2012) 1161–1169.

[22]Y. C. Lien and I. Filatotchev, Ownership characteristics as determinants of FDI location decisions in emerging economies, *Journal of World Business*, **50** (2015) 637–650.

[23]G. Savoiu and M. Taicu, Foreign direct investment models, based on country risk for some post-socialist central and Eastern European Economies, *Procedia Economics and Finance*, **10** (2014) 249–260.

[24]D. Holland and N. Pain, The determinants and impact of foreign direct investment in the transition economies: a panel data analysis, in V. Edwards, ed., *Convergence or Divergence: Aspirations and Reality in Central and Eastern Europe and Russia, Proceedings 4th Annual conference, Centre for Research into East European Business* (University of Buckingham, 1998).

real interest rates, inflation rate, and domestic investment.[25] It should be highlighted that Naveed and Shabbir found trade openness is significant and positively affecting GDP per capita growth in 23 developed countries within the period of 1971–2000.[26]

Jadhav explored FDI determinants in BRICS countries taking into account market size, trade openness, natural resources and inflation rate, political stability/no violence, government effectiveness, regulatory quality, control of corruption, voice and accountability, and rule of law.[27]

Sandhu and Fredericks included to the model in their attempt to reveal determinants of FDI in Malaysia the following variables: market size, infrastructure, workforce, political stability, firm expertise and reputation, firm experience, firm size, investment behavior that conforms to the follow-the-leader theory.[28]

8.4.2 *Impact of FDI on Economic Growth Approach Literature*

A vast number of researches have been conducted on a group country level as well as on a national level in order to define the exact effect of FDI on economic growth. Consecutively, the received study results are divergent, relying on financial and economic conditions of a country.

Likewise, Hanousek *et al.* summarized the broad range of empirical results on direct effects and spillover effects of FDI drawn from 21 studies focusing on transition countries.[29] Teker *et al.* investigated the trends and dispersion of FDIs in Asian and European transition

---

[25] I. Cevis and B. Camurdan, The economic determinants of foreign direct investment in developing countries and transition economies, *The Pakistan Development Review*, **46** (3) (2007) 285–299.

[26] A. Naveed and G. Shabbir, Trade openness, FDI and economic growth: A panel study, *Pakistan Economic and Social Review*, **XLIV** (1) (2006) 137–154.

[27] P. Jadhav, Determinants of foreign direct investment in BRICS economies: Analysis of economic, institutional and political factor, *Procedia — Social and Behavioral*, **37** (2012) 5–14.

[28] M. S. Sandhu and L. J. Fredericks, Factors influencing foreign direct investment in the Malaysian services sector: A theoretical framework, *UNITAR E-Journal*, **1** (1) (2005) 8–31.

[29] J. Hanousek, E. Kocenda and M. Maurel, Direct and indirect effects of FDI in emerging European markets: A survey and meta-analysis, *Economic Systems*, **35** (2011) 301–322.

economies for the period of 1992–2011.[30] Lyroudi *et al.* revealed that FDI does not exhibit any significant impact on economic growth in the transition economies.[31]

Khan and Mehboob examined the effects of FDI Inflows on GDP from 1992 to 2010 of 59 countries. The empirical analysis indicates a significant positive relationship Gross Domestic Product (GDP) and FDI Inflows.[32]

Borensztein *et al.* tested the effect of FDI on economic growth for 69 developing countries. The study findings reveal that FDI contributes to economic growth only when advanced technologies are available in the host economy.[33]

Moudatsou and Kyrkilis examined the causal order between inward FDI and economic growth for EU (European Union) and ASEAN (Association of South Eastern Asian Nations) over the period, 1970–2003.[34]

Tiwari and Mutascu examined the impact of FDI on economic growth in Asian countries for the period 1986–2008. They found that both FDI and exports enhance the growth process.[35]

Gudaro *et al.* analyzed the impact of FDI in Pakistan for the period, 1981–2010.[36]

---

[30] S. Teker, H. Tuzla and A. Pala, Foreign direct investments: Asian and European Transition Economies, *International Journal of Economics and Finanaial Issues*, **4** (1) (2014) 71–82.

[31] K. Lyroudi, J. Papanastasiou and A. Vamvakidis, Foreign direct investment and economic growth in transition economies, *South Eastern Europe Journal of Economics*, **1** (2004) 97–110.

[32] S. Khan and F. Mehboob, Impact of FDI on GDP: An analysis of global economy on production function, *MPRA Paper*, No. 55352 (2014), p. 14.

[33] E. Borensztein, J. De Gregorio and J.-W. Lee, How does foreign direct investment affect economic growth?, *Journal of International Economics*, **45** (1997) 115–135.

[34] A. Moudatsou and D. Kyrkilis, FDI and economic growth: Causality for the EU and ASEAN, *Journal of Economic Integration*, **26** (3) (2011) 554–577.

[35] A. K. Tiwari, Mutascu and Mihai, Economic growth and FDI in Asia: A panel-data approach, *Economic Analysis & Policy*, **41** (2) (2011) 173–187.

[36] A. M. Gudaro, I. U. Chhapra and S. A. Sheikh, Impact of foreign direct investment on economic growth: A case study of Pakistan, *Journal of Management and Social Sciences*, **8** (2) (2012) 22–30.

Notwithstanding, Iqbal *et al.* revealed that Pakistan Economic Growth capacity depends upon its ability to attract FDI and degree of FDI impact on GDP depends upon its trade policy regime, that is, export promotion policy.

Antwi and Zhao studied the relationship between FDI and economic growth in Ghana for the period, 1980–2010. The study results indicate a long-run negative relationship between GDP and FDI.[37]

Hoang *et al.* examined the effects of the FDI on economic growth in Vietnam for the years, 1995–2006. The study findings show a strong and positive effect of FDI on economic growth in Vietnam as a channel of increasing the stock of capital.[38] Malhotra examined the impact of FDI on the Indian economy. In the case of India, FDI has had a positive impact on economic growth.[39]

There are few researches which conducted analysis on the empirical literature. In this setting, Iwasaki and Tokunaga *et al.* conducted analysis of the literature that empirically examines the impact of FDI on economic growth in Central and Eastern Europe and the former Soviet Union. They found that existing studies indicate a growth-enhancing effect of FDI in the region as a whole.[40] In addition to this, Iamsiraroj and Ulubasoglu explored the global FDI–growth relationship through an "informed" econometric analysis predicated on substantial guidance obtained from a detailed investigation of 880 estimates reported in 108 published studies. They identified that appropriate absorptive

---

[37]S. Antwi and Z. Xicang, Impact of foreign direct investment and economic growth in Ghana: A cointegration analysis, *International Journal of Business and Social Research (IJBSR)*, **3** (1) (2013) 64–74.

[38]T. T. Hoang, P. Wiboonchutikula and B. Tubtimtong, Does foreign direct investment promote economic growth in Vietnam?. *ASEAN Economic Bulletin*, **27** (3) (2010) 295–311.

[39]B. Malhotra, Foreign direct investment: Impact on Indian economy, *Global Journal of Business Management and Information Technology*, **4** (1) (2014) 17–23.

[40]I. Iwasaki and M. Tokunaga, Macroeconomic impacts of FDI in transition economies: A meta-analysis, *World Development*, **61** (2014) 53–69.

capacity indicators for affirmative growth are trade openness and financial development rather than schooling.[41]

8.5 Methods

8.5.1 *Data and Case Selection*

The World Bank Indicator Report, The National Statistics of the Kyrgyz Republic Reports, Reports of the National Bank of the Kyrgyz Republic serve as the major sources of data in this study.

We conducted an empirical model to investigate the determinants of inward FDI in the Kyrgyz Republic first and then the effect of FDI on economic growth. The following research questions are raised in the study:

- There is a significant impact of selected FDI determinants on inward FDI;
- There is a significant impact of FDI on economic growth.

8.5.2 *Empirical Model and Hypotheses*

Based on the literature, we have designed the determinants of FDI. For analyzing the specific effects of determinants of inward FDI in Kyrgyzstan for the period of 1993–2014, we have specified the following (multiple linear regression) models:

- **The first model:**

$$\text{FDI} = \beta_0 + \beta_1 \log(\text{GDP}) - \beta_2 \log(\text{GNI}) + \beta_3 \text{Infl} - \beta_4 \text{Exchrate} - \beta_5 \text{TotRes} - \beta_6 \text{Tax} + \beta_7 \text{Tropen} + \beta_8 \text{Unempl} - \beta_9 \text{Polst} + \beta_{10} \text{Invfr} - \beta_{11} \text{Techn} + \beta_{12} \log(\text{Laborforce}) + u.$$

[41] S. Iamsiraroj and M. A. Ulubasoglu, Foreign direct investment and economic growth: A real relationship or wishful thinking? *Economic Modelling*, **51** (2015) 200–213.

- **The second model:**

$$FDI = \beta0 + \beta1\log(GDP) - \beta2\log(GNI) + \beta3Infl - \beta4Exchrate + \beta5Unempl - \beta6\ Techn + u,$$

where FDI represents the foreign direct investment net inflows, log(GDP) the gross domestic product growth in logs, log(GNI) the gross national income in logs, Infl the rate of inflation in %, Exchrate the exchange rate in local currency units per US dollar, TotRes the total reserves, Tax the tax revenue, percent of GDP, Tropen the trade openness, Unempl the rate of unemployment in %, Polst the political stability index, Invfr the investment freedom index, Techn the technicians as a percent of total R&D personnel, Log (Labor force) the labor force, in logs, and u is the error term, which represents factors other than the independent variables that affect the dependent one.

In the above model, FDI is the dependent variable, whereas other variables are independent. Some variables are transformed to log. It converts the nonlinear parameters into a linear one. The econometric model is estimated by using time-series data approach.

The coefficients that are interpreted in a linear regression model represent the following: the derivatives of Y with respect to each of the X variables. They measure how much Y changes for one-unit changes in the X variables.

Investigation of p-value is a fast way to reach the conclusion that we otherwise would receive by carrying out all the steps in the test of significance approach or the confidence interval approach. The p-value demonstrates if the parameter is significantly different from zero or not:

- If the p-value is equal to or greater than the specified significance level, H1 is concluded.
- If the p-value is less than the specified significance level, H1 is concluded.

Since the p-value for the intercept is larger than any conventional significance levels, say 5%, we cannot reject the null hypothesis that the intercept is different from zero. On the other hand, for the slope coefficient, the p-value is much smaller than 5% and therefore, we can reject the null hypothesis and conclude that it is significantly different from zero.

8.6. Results and Interpretations

The findings of multiple linear regression model are presented in Table 8.2.

R-squared is the ratio of the explained variation compared to the total variation. The R-squared of the regression, sometimes called the coefficient of determination, is defined as

$$R^2 = SSE/SST = 1 - SSR/SST.$$

R-squared in the model equals to 0.8862 or 88.62%, which is the percentage of the response variable variation that is explained by a linear model. The higher the R-squared, the better the model fits our data, whereas adjusted R-squared gives the percentage of variation explained by only those independent variables that in reality affect the dependent variable. Adjusted R-squared = 0.7346 or 73.46%.

So, in the employed model, just GDP, GNI, and exchange rate conclude H1.

The first model in Table 8.2 shows that just these two factors have influence on FDI, and others have more than 5%. But if we take away some variables such as logLabor force, logTotal Reserves, Tax Revenue, logTrade openness, Political Stability, Investment Freedom, we obtain the second model in Table 8.3. All factors impact on FDI, except unemployment rate.

Table 8.4 demonstrates the correlations of all factors that influence FDI. According to the empirical results, inflation, exchange rate and technicians have a negative relation with FDI.

According to the results of the conducted research, we can conclude that the most significant factors affecting the volume of inward FDI are as follows:

- GDP,
- GNI,
- Inflation,
- Exchange rate,
- Technicians.

Table 8.2: The Findings of Multiple Linear Regression Model.

Source	ss	df	Ms	
Model	8.4265e+17	12	7.0221e+16	Number of obs. = 22
Residual	1.0816e+17	9	1.2017e+16	F (12,9) = 5.84
Total	9.5080e+17	21	4.5276e+16	Prob > F = 0.0063
				R-squared = 0.8862
				Adj. R-squared = 0.7346
				Root MSE = 1.1e+08

FDI	Coeff.	Std. Err	Y	$P > |t|$	[95% Conf. Interval]	
logGDP	5.01e+09	1.43e+09	3.51	0.007	1.78e+09	8.24e+09
logGNI	-4.77e+09	1.51e+09	-3.16	0.012	-8.19e+09	-1.36e+09
Infl	317 198.8	568668.8	0.56	0.591	-969219.5	1603617
logLaborfo~e	4.66e+08	2.90e+09	0.16	0.876	-6.09e+09	7.02e+09
Exchangera~r	-1.50e+07	6017439	-2.49	0.035	-2.86e+07	-1355302

logTotal Re~s	−1.79e+07	9.65e+07	−0.19	0.857	−2.36e+08	2.01e+08
Tax revenue~P	−4989778	4900539	−1.02	0.335	−1.61e+07	6096011
logTradeop~s	2.83e+07	6.76e+07	0.42	0.685	−1.25e+08	1.81e+08
Unemployme~e	2.27e+07	1.55e+07	1.46	0.177	−1.24e+07	5.78e+07
Politicals~2	−3.23e+07	7.06e+07	−0.46	0.658	−1.92e+08	1.27e+08
Investment~m	2926423	5452221	0.54	0.604	−9407358	1.53e+07
Technician~p	−1.33e+07	9548596	−1.40	0.196	−3.49e+07	8268224
_cons	−7.78e+09	1.56e+10	−0.50	0.629	−4.30e+10	2.74e+10

Table 8.3: The Findings of Multiple Linear Regression Model.

Source	ss	df	Ms	Number of obs. = 22	
Model	8.2631e+17	6	1.3772e+17	F (6,15) = 16.59	
				Prob > F = 0.0000	
Residual	1.2449e+17	15	8.2993e+15	R-squared = 0.8691	
				Adj. R-squared = 0.8167	
Total	9.5080e+17	21	4.5276e+16	Root MSE = 9.1e+07	

FDI	Coeff.	Std. Err	t	$P > |t|$	[95% Conf. Interval]	
logGDP	5.15e+09	1.06e+09	4.84	0.000	2.88e+09	7.42e+9
logGNI	-4.86e+09	1.06e+09	-4.57	0.000	-7.13e+09	-2.59e+09

FDI	Coeff.	Std. Err	Y	$P > |t|$	[95% Conf. Interval]	
Infl	412818.4	167783.8	2.46	0.026	55195.66	770441.1
Exchangera~r	-1.39e+07	2914124	-4.78	0.000	-2.01e+07	-7725708
Unemployme~e	1.89e+07	1.15e+07	1.65	0.121	-5591338	4.34e+07
Technician~p	-1.69e+07	6785017	-2.49	0.025	-3.13e+07	-2409435
_cons	-4.88e+09	6.43e+08	-7.59	0.000	-6.25e+09	-3.51e+09

Table 8.4: The Correlations of all Factors that Influence FDI.

	FDI	logGDP	logGNI	Infl	Exchan~r	Techni~p
FDI	1.0000					
log*GDF*	0.6603	1.0000				
log*GNI*	0.6561	0.9998	1.0000			
Infl	−0.2239	−0.6212	−0.6188	1.0000		
Exchangera~r	0.3735	0.8709	0.8683	−0.5538	1.0000	
Technician~p	−0.0237	0.2570	0.2502	−0.4028	0.3240	1.0000

8.7 FDI Impact on Economic Growth

Since the average level of inward FDI to GDP is only 4.61% and as a result of empirical study, changes in GDP, GNI, inflation, exchange rate, technicians as a percent of total R&D personnel are the utmost determinants of inward FDI. It is crucial to disclose the FDI influence on GDP.

The data statistics is taken from World Bank dataset and spans from 1993 to 2014. The dataset includes the following variables: GDP and the size of FDI (see Table 8.5). The aim of the employed model is to establish the possible relationship between the flow of FDI into the economy of the country and the rate of economic growth. In this model, the ratio of the two above-mentioned factors and their correlation value are demonstrated.

Table 8.5 demonstrates low percentage of *R*-squared, which shows the low level of FDI that constitutes the GDP.

The results of correlation analysis indicate a strong statistical relationship between indicators of economic growth and FDI inwards in the economy of the Kyrgyz Republic (see Table 8.6).

Source, ss, df, Ms

Table 8.5: The Findings of FDI's Impact on GDP.

Source	ss	df	Ms	
Model	1.2132e + 17	1	1.2132e + 17	Number of obs. = 22
				$F_{(1,20)} = 14.38$
				Prob. > F = 0.0011
Residual	1.6875e + 17	20	8.4377e + 15	R-squared = 0.4182
				Adj. R-squared = 0.3892
Total	2.9008e + 17	21	1.3813e + 16	Root MSE = 9.2e+07

GDP	Coeff.	Std. Err	t	$P > |t|$	[95% Conf. Interval]	
logFDI	4.70e + 07	1.24e + 07	3.79	0.001	2.11e + 07	7.28e + 07
_cons	−7.23e + 08	2.26e + 08	−3.20	0.005	−1.19e + 09	−2.52e + 08

Table 8.6: The Results of Correlation Analysis.

	GDP	log*FDI*
GDP	1.0000	
log*FDI*	0.6467	1.0000

8.8 Conclusion

FDI and trade are often seen as important catalysts for economic growth in the developing countries. FDI also stimulates domestic investment and facilitates improvements in human capital and institutions in the host countries. According to the study results, we conclude that the most significant determinants of inward FDI are GDP, GNI, inflation, exchange rate, technicians as a percent of total R&D personnel.

Furthermore, the study results demonstrate that there is a very strong positive correlation between FDI and GDP and this relationship is statistically significant for the Kyrgyz Republic.

The presented empirical study results show a crucial role for policymakers of the transition economy of the Kyrgyz Republic to undertake the utmost and valid macroeconomic policy in the country to attract FDI.

CHAPTER 9

China–Kyrgyzstan Railway Meets IDE–GSM

**S. Kumagai, I. Isono, S. Keola, K. Hayakawa,
T. Gokan and K. Tsubota**

Institute of Developing Economies, Japan

9.1 Introduction

As a project of the Belt and Road (B&R) Initiative, the construction of a new rail link from China to Uzbekistan via Kyrgyzstan is planned.[1] Our focus is on the link between Kashgar, China, and Karasuu, Kyrgyzstan near Osh in the connection between Uzbekistan and China. This link is designed to provide a shortcut to send goods from Yiwu, China to Tehran, Iran, and transit fees for Kyrgyzstan. Since the link will pass only through Southern Kyrgyzstan, it may not provide positive benefits in Northern Kyrgyzstan. Thus, it is worth examining the impact of the new railroad on the economic activities in various regions of Kyrgyzstan.

For that purpose, we used an Institute of Developing Economies– Geographical Simulation Model (IDE–GSM) which is a simulation model

---

[1] J. Farchy and J. Kynge, New trade routes: silk road corridor, map: Connecting central Asia A ribbon of road, rail and energy projects to help increase trade, *Financial Times*, 10 May. Available at: https://www.ft.com/content/ee5cf40a-15e5-11e6-9d98-00386a18 e39d (accessed on 13 December 2016).

based on Spatial Economics and New Economic Geography. Different from a cost–benefit analysis, the IDE–GSM calculates only the long-term benefits derived from the improvement of trade and transport facilitation measures (TTFMs) via the dynamics of population and industries. In the model, the spatial configuration of economic activities is determined by the balance between the centrifugal and dispersion forces. The model contains positive feedback between supply and demand for consumption goods and intermediate goods as the centrifugal force, whereas regarding the dispersion force, the demand for consumption goods exists in remote areas in the model.

Since the IDE–GSM contains 2,063 regions and 89 countries, the results we obtained were not only for Kyrgyzstan and China, but also for the neighboring countries. Furthermore, the transport costs for sending goods between regions in the IDE–GSM could be divided into transport costs, time costs, export tariff, import tariff, and non-tariff barriers. We also examined the impact of customs facilitation at the border between China and Kyrgyzstan, as additional policy measures may be needed to exploit the benefit from the railway construction.

The remainder of this chapter is organized as follows. Section 9.2 introduces how we prepare for our analysis. Section 9.3 explains two scenarios and the results of their numerical analyses. Section 9.4 concludes the chapter.

9.2   China–Kyrgyzstan–Uzbekistan Railway

The sentiment to construct the China–Kyrgyzstan–Uzbekistan Railway resulted in technical and environmental investigations to assess the development of the railroads between Bishkek and Kashgar.[2]

Data for the new railway used in this chapter were borrowed from TRACECA (see Footnote 2), which was added into the United Nations[3]

---

[2]TRACECA, EU-TACIS feasibility study of new rail links between the Ferghana Valley, Bishkek and Kashgar, EU TACIS Final report 2003, Volume 1, Executive Summary (2003). Available at: http://www.traceca-org.org/fileadmin/fm-dam/TAREP/32la/file-group/vol.0-5_english/volume_1.pdf (accessed on 13 December 2016).

[3]United Nations, Euro-Asian Transport linkages: Paving the way for a more efficient Euro-Asian transport, Phase II, Expert Group Report, UN Economic Commission for Europe (2003). Available at https://www.unece.org/fileadmin/DAM/trans/main/eatl/docs/EATL_Report_Phase_II.pdf (accessed on 13 December 2016).

data to fix the transport route, distance, and time, and enlarge the existing dataset of IDE–GSM. That is, the route and distance connecting Kashgar, Trougart, Uzgen, and Karasuu in TRACECA (see Footnote 3) were used. However, the speed was based on TRACECA (see Footnote 3).

9.3 Economic Impacts of the New Railway

To analyze the economic impacts, we prepared a dataset from 2010 to run the IDE–GSM (see Appendix) as the first step. Then, running a numerical analysis with the IDE–GSM, we obtained a dataset for the year 2030 assuming the absence of new infrastructure projects and custom facilitation. Finally, assuming the construction of the new railway and/or facilitating custom procedures in 2020, the IDE–GSM numerical analysis was performed, which yielded a dataset for 2030 that reflected the impact of the new railway and/or custom facilitation. The economic impacts were measured using the data from the 2030 simulation obtained via the IDE–GSM by subtracting the data impacted by the construction of the new railways and/or custom facilitation from the data without such impacts. In other words, positive (negative) results indicated that the values obtained by numerical analysis with the new railway and/or customs facilitation were larger (smaller) than that without them (see Figure 9.1).

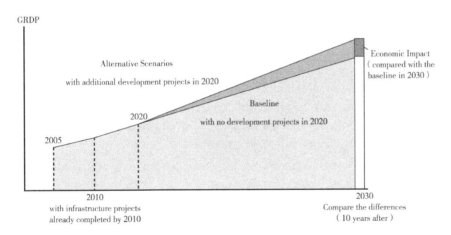

Figure 9.1:   The Approach used to Estimate the Impacts in IDE–GSM.
Source: Authors.

9.3.1 Scenario 1

This scenario examines the impact of connecting Kashgar, Trougart, Uzgen, and Karasuu by train without customs facilitation measures at the national border between China and Kyrgyzstan.

The region with the highest benefit was found to be the area in Kyrgyzstan near the national border between China and Kyrgyzstan. The positive impact was found only in Southern Kyrgyzstan. The numerical analysis showed that these areas would benefit both from an increase in population and real GDP. However, within Southern Kyrgyzstan, the GDP in Batken, which is located in the western part of Kyrgyzstan and in the area surrounded by Tajikistan, was found to be constant, and the population in Batken was shown to decrease. Thus, the per capita GDP was found to increase slightly in these areas. The results for Chuy, which is located in the northern part of Kyrgyzstan near Kazakhstan along with the capital of Kyrgyzstan, Bishkek, were found to be almost the same as those for Batken. The drawbacks associated with building the new railway emerged only in Talas, which is located in the northwestern part of Kyrgyzstan near Kazakhstan, since both population and real GDP were shown to decrease. For Kyrgyzstan, this seems beneficial considering the fact that negative impacts are expected to emerge in only a single region out of seven. However, resources to effectively narrow this gap must be concentrated in Talas.

The numerical analysis shows that both population and real GDP increased in such a way that the per capita GDP in Kashgar increased at a negligible rate.

The positive impact was visible in Tibet near India, owing to the increase in population and real GDP.

It can be seen that the impact of connecting Kashgar, Trougart, Uzgen, and Karasuu would be limited around the new railway project by measuring the impact on the scale in the legend.

9.3.2 Scenario 2

This scenario examines the impact of connecting Kashgar, Trougart, Uzgen, and Karasuu by train with custom facilitation measures at the national border between China and Kyrgyzstan.

The contrast between the winners and the losers became clearer by facilitating customs additionally. Furthermore, many regions would benefit from the positive impacts.

A larger area is impacted as a result of migration and trade. Positive impacts can be seen in Uzbekistan, Turkmenistan, southwestern Kazakhstan, and almost all of Russia and Mongolia, whereas negative impacts can be observed in regions near the Caspian Sea in Russia.

The positive impacts covered a larger area in China and Russia, and even in regions of Korea and Japan. However, the scale of such impacts was not found to be large and there was hardly any impact in Kazakhstan and South Asia. The negative impacts were shown to exist in the eastern part of Mongolia, the western part of Nepal, the area near Caspian Sea, and also the area facing the Barents Sea in Russia.

9.4 Conclusion

We examined the impact of connecting Kashgar, Trougart, Uzgen, and Karasuu and facilitating customs at the national border between China and Kyrgyzstan.

We found that the railway connection was projected to have a positive impact in Southern Kyrgyzstan and a negative impact in regions of Northern Kyrgyzstan, neither of which is the capital city of Kyrgyzstan. The contrast between the regions where the per capita GDP was found to increase and decrease became clear when customs facilitation as included in the analysis. Furthermore, we found that China, most in Central Asia countries, and almost all regions of Russia and Mongolia would benefit from both a new railway project and customs facilitation, although the scale of such benefits would be small.

Since the region predicted to suffer from the new railway only included one region in Krygzstan out of seven, transferring resources from the benefiting regions to the suffering region may be sufficient to narrow regional gaps.

Appendix

Since 2007, a numerical simulation with a general equilibrium model based on NEG, IDE–GSM has been developed for numerical analyses of the impacts of TTFMs at a subnational level. Our model comprises eight economic sectors, including manufacturing and non-manufacturing sectors, and more than 2,000 regions in 18 countries/economies in East Asia and CWA countries, Russia and Mongolia. The East Asian countries/economies include Bangladesh, Brunei Darussalam, Cambodia, China, Hong Kong, India, Indonesia, Japan, Korea, Lao PDR, Macao, Myanmar, Malaysia, Philippines, Singapore, Taiwan, Thailand, and Vietnam. IDE–GSM was developed as a strand of the Core-Periphery Model of Krugman[4] and Fujita *et al.*,[5] with two main objectives, namely, (1) to simulate the dynamics of the locations of populations and industries in East Asia over the long term, and, (2) to analyze the impact of specific TTFMs on regional economies at subnational levels. In our simulation model, more than 2,000 regions were included. There were two endowments: labor and land. Labor is mobile within a country, but prohibited to migrate to other countries at this moment. Land is unequally spread across all regions and jointly owned by all labors of the region.

All products in the three sectors are tradeable. Transport costs are supposed to be of the iceberg type, for example, assume that one unit of product is sent from one region to another, the unit arrives with less than one portion. Depending on the lost portion, the supplier sets a higher price. The increase in price compared to the producer's price is regarded as the transport cost. Transport costs within the same region are considered negligible.

The simulation procedures are as follows. First, with given distributions of employment and regional GDP by sectors and regions according to the actual data, short-run equilibrium is obtained. Observing the achieved equilibrium, workers migrate among regions and industries according to the differences in the real wages. Workers move to the sectors that offer higher real wage rates in the same region, and move to the regions that offer higher real wages within the same country. We obtain the new distribution of workers and economic activities. With this new distribution and

---

[4]P. Krugman, Increasing returns and economic geography, *Political Economy*, 99 (1991) 483–499.

[5]M. Fujita, P. Krugman and A. J. Venables, *The Spatial Economy: Cities, Regions and International Trade* (MIT Press, Cambridge, MA, 1999).

predicted population growth, the next short-run equilibrium is obtained for a following year, and we observe migration again. These computations are repeated for typically 20 years, i.e., from the year 2010 to 2030.

Primarily based on official statistics, we derived the Gross Regional Product (GRP) for the agriculture sector, mining sector, five manufacturing sectors, and the service sector. The manufacturing sector was divided into five subsectors — food processing, garments and textiles, electronics, automotive, and other manufacturing industries. The population and area of arable land for each region were compiled from official statistical sources.

The number of routes included in the simulation was more than 10,000 (land: 6,500, sea: 950, air: 2,050 and railway: 450). The route data consisted of start city, end city, distance between the cities, speed of the vehicle running on the route, etc. The land routes between cities were based mainly on the "Asian Highway" database of the United Nations Economic and Social Commission for Asia and the Pacific (UNESCAP). The actual road distances between cities were used; if the road distances were not available, the distances between cities in a straight line were employed. The data on air and sea routes are compiled from Nihon Kaiun Shukaijo[6] and the dataset assembled by the team of the Logistics Institute-Asia Pacific (TLIAP), and 950 sea routes and 2,050 air routes were selectively included in the model. The railway data were adopted from various sources, such as maps and official websites of railway companies.

The industry-related parameters are provided in Table A.1. We mainly adopted the elasticity of substitution for the manufacturing sectors from Hummels[7] and estimated it for services. Estimates for the elasticity of services were obtained from the estimation of the usual gravity equations for trade services, including such independent variables as the importer's GDP, exporter's GDP, importer's corporate tax, geographical distance between countries, a dummy for FTAs, linguistic commonality dummy, and a colonial dummy. For this estimation, we mainly employed data from the "Organisation for Economic Co-operation and Development Statistics on International Trade in Services."

---

[6]N. K. Shukaijo, Japanese Shipping Exchange *Distance Tables for World Shipping*, 8th edn. (1983).

[7]D. Hummels, Toward a geography of trade costs. GTAP Working Paper No. 17 (1999).

Table A.1: Industry Parameters.

Item	Consumption Share	Labor Input Share	Elasticity of Substitution
Agriculture	0.04	0.61	—
Automotive	0.02	0.57	7.10
E&E	0.02	0.57	8.80
Textile	0.01	0.64	8.40
Food	0.03	0.61	5.10
Oth. Mfg.	0.16	0.59	5.30
Services	0.70	1.00	3.00

Source: Authors' calculations. Elasticity of substitution is mainly adopted from Hummels (1999).

The consumption share of consumers by industry was uniformly determined for the entire region in the model. It would be more realistic to change the share by country or region, but we could not do so because of a lack of sufficiently reliable consumption data at a finer level of the geographical unit. The single labor input share for each industry was uniformly applied throughout the entire region and time period in the model. Although it may differ among countries/regions and across time, we used an "average" value, in this case, the value for Thailand, which is a country in the middle-stage of economic development and whose value was taken from the Asian International Input–Output Table for 2005 by the IDE–JETRO. For the manufacturing sector data source, we used the survey conducted by the JETRO.[8]

The transport parameters are listed in Table A.2. Our transport costs comprised the physical transport costs, time costs, tariff rates, and non-tariff barriers. The physical transport costs were a function of the distance traveled, travel speed per hour, physical travel cost per kilometer, and holding costs for domestic/international transshipments at border crossings, stations, ports, or airports. The time costs depended on travel distance, travel speed per hour, time cost per hour, and holding times for

---

[8] JETRO, Zai-Azia-Oseania Nikkei Kigyo Gittai Chosa (2013). Available at http://www.jetro.go.jp/j.le/report/07001539/0700153901a.pdf

Table A.2: Transport Parameters by Mode.

Item	Truck	Rail	Sea	Air	Unit
Cost/Kim	1	0.5	0.24	45.2	US$/km
Avg. Speed	38.5	19.1	14.7	800	km/hour
Transit Time (Dom.)	0	2.7	3.3	2.2	Hours
Transit Time (Intl.)	13.2	13.2	15	12.8	Hours
Transit Cost (Dom.)	0	0	190	690	US$
Transit Cost (Intl.)	500	500	491	1276	US$

Source: Estimated by Authors.

domestic/international transshipments at border crossings, stations, ports, or airports. These parameters were derived from the ASEAN Logistics Network Map 2008 by the JETRO and by estimating the model of the firm-level transport mode choice with the "Establishment Survey on Innovation and Production Network" (ERIA) for 2008 and 2009, which includes manufacturers in Indonesia, Philippines, Thailand, and Vietnam.

Based on these parameters, we calculated the sum of physical transport and time costs for all possible routes between two regions. Employing the Floyd–Warshall algorithm for determining the optimal route and transport mode of each region and good,[9] we obtained the sum of physical transport and time costs for each pairing of the two regions by industry. The procedures to calculate these parameters are explained in Kumagai *et al.*[10]

Further Reading

Foreign & Commonwealth Office, The China–Kyrgyzstan–Uzbekistan Railway Project. [MS word] Foreign Office research analyst papers published 5 June 2014, Available at https://www.gov.uk/government/uploads/system/uploads/attachment_data/.le/317670/China-Kyrgyzstan-Uzbekistan_Railway_project. doc (accessed on 13 December 2016).

---

[9]T. H. Cormen, C. E. Leiserson, R. L. Rivest and S. Clifford, *Introduction to Algorithms* (MIT Press, 2001).

[10]S. Kumagai, K. Hayakawa, I. Isono, S. Keola and K. Tsubota, Geographical simulation analysis for logistics enhancement in Asia, *Economic Modelling*, 34 (2013) 145–153.

CHAPTER 10

An Analysis of the China–Pakistan Economic Corridor (CPEC) and Its Prospects

Ahmad Rashid Malik

Institute of Strategic Studies, Islamabad, Pakistan

10.1 Introduction

In today's geopolitics, the China–Pakistan Economic Corridor (CPEC) draws huge attention. Reports, analyses, and opinion pieces are written across the globe. There are positive analyses as well as negative analyses. Most of the analyses are on politics and not on economics. The subject has become popular among scholars of International Relations, Political Science, Security Studies, etc. In this context, the CPEC is the most discussed and debated project in current history. In spite of entertaining a large number of political analyses, contradictory views, and concerns, the Governments of Pakistan and China are, however, strongly committed to going ahead with the CPEC and continuously striving hard to make it a successful bilateral economic model for both and other countries.

This chapter is not on the politics of the CPEC as it is widely discussed. Rather, it analyzes the political economy of the CPEC with a focus on economic fundamentals of the CPEC to see how viable the CPEC is for the economy of Pakistan in concrete terms instead of discussing regional and global political concerns of the CPEC.

The CPEC is a pilot and the flagship project of the Belt and Road (B&R) Initiative that aimed to build a number of economic corridors. President Xi Jinping considers Pakistan as an important partner of the B&R Initiative. The idea of the B&R Initiative was expounded by President Xi Jinping when he visited Kazakhstan in September 2013 and Indonesia in October the same year. The B&R Initiative is actually the new name of the ancient Silk Road, connecting China with Central Asia, the Middle East, and onward to Europe some 2,500 years ago. China is a home and a starting point of the Silk Road.

The basic idea behind the B&R Initiative is to revive the ancient Silk Road that had facilitated trade, discoveries, cultural cohesion, and cross civilizational bonds among nations in the past. At least six economic corridors have been designed under the B&R Initiative at the moment, namely:

(1) China–Central & West Asia Economic Corridor
(2) China–Pakistan Economic Corridor
(3) Bangladesh–China–India–Myanmar Economic Corridor
(4) China–Indonesia Peninsula Economic Corridor
(5) China–Mongolia–Russia Economic Corridor
(6) New-Eurasia Land Bridge Economic Corridor

The major focus of the B&R Initiative is on the following areas: policy coordination, connectivity, unimpeded trade, financial integration, and people-to-people bond.[1] Of these six important economic corridors, the CPEC was an early starter and it is to be considered a pilot and flagship project of the B&R Initiative whose success would determine the feasibility of all other economic corridors.

The CPEC has historical reasons. The CPEC was offered by China to Pakistan five months earlier when Premier Li Keqiang visited Pakistan in

---

[1] National Development and Reform Commission, Ministry of foreign Affairs, and Ministry of Commerce, People's Republic of China, with State Council Authorization, *Vision and Actions on Jointly Building Silk Road Economic Belt and 21st-Century Maritime Silk Road* (Foreign Languages Press, Beijing, 2015), pp. 12–24.

May 2013. Even the proposal for oil and gas pipeline between the two countries was discussed much earlier to 2013. The decision to construct the Gwadar Deep Sea Port during the visit of Premier Zhu Rongji in 2001 led to building of land route and oil and gas pipeline between Gwadar and Kashgar.[2] Further, some would suggest that the Karakoram Highway (KKH), built during 1956–1978, was the main motivating factor for Pakistan–China land route cooperation. Therefore, there are historical reasons behind the CPEC under the Pakistan–China lasting cooperation.

The progress on the CPEC projects is going well. Chinese Government has made CPEC a part of its 13th Five-Year Plan (2016–2020) and many early harvest projects will be completed by 2018–2020, which will give a new boost to CPEC projects to be undertaken in the second phase up to 2030.

This chapter highlights the unimpeded trade and regional connectivity and sees its benefits for the economy of Pakistan.

10.2 Unimpeded Trade

Traditionally, economic and trade relations between Pakistan and China had remained extremely low. The decade-wise trade between the two countries was recorded as shown in Table 10.1.

Table 10.1: Pakistan–China Bilateral Decade-Wise Trade 1960–2010 (US$ Million).

Decade	Trade
1960	18.3
1970	73.4
1980	401.6
1990	424.6
2000	722.1
2010	10.854.7

Source: IMF: Direction of Trade Statistics. Washington: International Monetary Fund, 2015 (Various years).

---

[2]L. Shulin, China–Pakistan Economic Corridor: A flagship and exemplary project of the "Belt and Road", *Strategic Studies*, **34 & 35** (4 & 1) (2014 and 2015) 165.

Table 10.2: Pakistan–China Bilateral Trade 2011–2014 (US$ Million).

Year	Trade
2011	11,211.6
2012	13,061.14
2013	15,033.02
2014	17,082

Source: IMF: Direction of Trade Statistics. Washington: International Monetary Fund, 2015 (Various years).

Bilateral trade was hardly US$ 424 million in 1990 that only increased to US$ 722 million in 2000. In 2007, both countries have signed the Free Trade Agreement (FTA) to boost bilateral trade, which stood at US$ 7.5 billion at that point. The FTA is now in the second phase, which will remove duties up to 90%. Therefore, a free trading regime would emerge between the two countries under the CPEC perspective.

Since the cultivation of strong diplomatic and defense ties, economic relations have not been at any realizable point. After the signing of the FTA and inauguration of the CPEC, bilateral trade is turning around and reached US$ 17 billion in 2014. At present, bilateral trade reaches US$ 19 billion mark (Table 10.2).[3]

At the moment, Pakistan imports more from China and exports less than three times to China. The largest trade deficit is also with China accumulating to over US$ 9 billion now. The Government is devising strategies to increase Pakistan's exports to China.

Meanwhile, when bilateral trade just turned around, the CPEC was inaugurated on 20 April 2015 following the President Xi Jinping's visit to Pakistan. At that time, as many as 51 agreements worth US$ 46 billion were signed. Most of the agreements were related to energy projects worth US$ 35 billion aiming to generate 10,400 MW electricity.

---

[3] Sino-Pak bilateral trade reaches dollar 18.9 billion: Chinese ambassador, *Pakistan Today (Islamabad)*, 28 September 2016.

However, the CPEC has the capacity to lower Pakistan's trade deficit and boost its exports to China for a variety of reasons especially when shortage of electricity in Pakistan would be decreased following the inauguration of energy projects next year and some the following year. Therefore, the greater impact of the CPEC would be on Pakistan's trade with China and also with other countries.

Furthermore, the CPEC is converting Pakistan into a "Transit State" in South Asia catering to the needs of China, Afghanistan, and Central Asia, and may be even Russia which had a long-cherished desire to reach warm water ports of the Arabian Sea during the Cold War but was hampered by a number of difficulties. Mongolia could also take advantage of Gwadar Port. When more oil would be exported to China via the Gulf and Iran, a major source of Chinese oil imports, it could boost Pakistan's trade indirectly. A pipeline will also be built from Gwadar to Kashgar to transport oil from the Persian Gulf and Iran. The emerging Pakistan under the CPEC would be a "gateway" to China and Central Asia. Additionally, CPEC would also boost regional trade. The results are in the pipeline.

Pakistan exported goods worth US$ 5.7 billion and imported goods worth US$ 18.9 billion in 2014, thus making the total trade of US$ 24.6 billion (Table 10.3). New trading infrastructure and industrial zones would drastically increase Pakistan's trade with these countries.

The future trade would be quadrupled with China taking the large chunk of Pakistan's trade in this region. Therefore, one point is clear that

Table 10.3: Pakistan's Regional Trade with Neighbors 2014 (US$ Million).

No	Country	Exports	Imports	Total
1	China	2,509	14,573	17,082
2	India	481	2,400	2,881
3	Iran	501	1,801	2,302
4	Afghanistan	2,222	195	2,417
Total		5,713	18,969	24,682

Source: IMF: Direction of Trade Statistics. Washington: International Monetary Fund, 2015 (Various years).

CPEC would boost bilateral trade between the two countries as well as regional trade. Solid bilateral trading ties are in the making.

Setting up of industrial zones is the backbone of the CPEC projects under the policy coordination between the two Governments.[4] The CPEC will give an unprecedented boost to build at least 29 industrial zones and 21 processing zones in different parts of Pakistan along the CPEC routes during the first phase of the projects.[5]

10.3 Economic Turnaround

The CPEC is a long-term comprehensive economic project. The package has boosted Pakistan's economy to a great extent within the past two years. The results are encouraging. The economic outlook of the economy has been changed. Economy has been showing positive trends. Many milestones have been achieved so far making it a vibrant and sustainable economy. The Government sets 5.7% growth rate for the next fiscal year.[6] International rating agencies have upgraded the trends of the economy of Pakistan. This included Japan External Trade Organization (JETRO), Standards & Poor's, Moody, and many other rating agencies. According to Morgan Stanley Capital International, Pakistan is becoming an emerging market because of the improvement in transparency, liquidity, and stock exchange.[7]

At present, the total Gross Domestic Product (GDP) of Pakistan is only US$ 269.7 billion.[8] It is a small GDP compared to other countries in Asia. The CPEC package of US$ 46 billion injected a new boost into Pakistan's GDP, which is around 17% of Pakistan's GDP. The CPEC

---

[4] L. Tong, CPEC industrial zones and China–Pakistan capacity cooperation, *Strategic Studies*, **34 & 35** (4 and 1) (Winter 2014–Spring 2015), 174–184.

[5] The Government proposes 29 industrial parks, 21 mineral zones under CPEC, *The News International* (*Rawalpindi*), 26 July 2015.

[6] Message from Minister for Finance, revenue, economic affairs, statistics and privatization, *Business Recorder* (*Islamabad*), 27 September 2016.

[7] Pakistan upgraded to emerging markets status, *The Express Tribune* (*Islamabad*), 15 July 2016.

[8] The World Bank, World Development Indicators Database, Available at http://databank.worldbank.org/data/download/GDP.pdf (accessed on 22 July 2016).

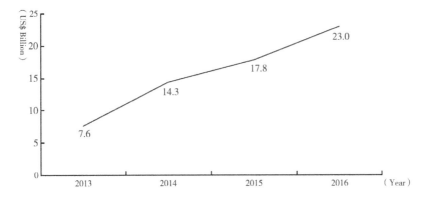

Figure 10.1: Pakistan's Foreign Reserves 2013–2016.

Source: The Global Economy. Available at: http://www/theglobaleconomy.com/Pakistan/Reserves/ & Daily Times (Lahore), 1 September 2016.

projects have been showing encouraging progress. Chinese companies have invested US$ 14 billion in the 30 Early Harvest Programs (EHPs), which are under construction.[9] Some of these projects are already completed and some are nearly completing within a year or so. The momentum of development of energy, roads, and infrastructure projects is built and is likely to continue after the EHP with much faster space.

Investment is an integral part of trade. The World Bank acknowledged Pakistan's growth. Ever since the CPEC has been offered to Pakistan, its foreign reserves have been showing an upward trend in the past three years. Pakistan's foreign reserves have climbed to US$ 23 billion at present (see Figure 10.1).

In addition to that, there would be workforce mobilization. The CPEC's projects would create at least 2 million new job opportunities.[10] The Multan–Sukker Motorway has created just over 10,000 jobs.[11] This is just an example. Every project has unprecedented job opportunities. This would also reduce unemployment and poverty in the country.

---

[9] China has so far invested $14 billion in 30 CPEC projects, see the statement of Zhao Lijian, Deputy Chief of Mission, Embassy of the People's Republic of China at Islamabad, *Pakistan Today (Islamabad)*, 28 September 2016.

[10] *The News International (Rawalpindi)* [Online], 5 July 2016.

[11] *Pakistan Today (Islamabad)*, 22 September 2016.

The CPEC package has a financial significance for Pakistan. As far as Pakistan's Foreign Direct Investment (FDI) is concerned, the CPEC package is the largest if one counted the entire FDI of Pakistan in the past 60 years received from all sources. The CPEC package is the biggest package ever offered to Pakistan by a foreign donor or an aid agency.[12] It is almost half of loans contracted by Pakistan since 1947. Now, under the CPEC, China has been massively investing in FDI in Pakistan during the last three years. Chinese FDI reached US$ 593.9 million in 2015–2016 and China has become Pakistan's largest FDI partner since the last three years.[13]

10.4 Regional Connectivity

The CPEC attracts huge regional attention. The CPEC is more about regional trade connectivity and transportation by providing a modern and efficient corridor for regional trade. The CPEC, in other words, is a symbol of trade connectivity.

It was not in the interest of British Imperial India, for instance, to promote trade between the Indian subcontinent and China and with other countries. By exporting opium from India into China in the 19th century, British virtually destroyed trade between the Indian subcontinent and China.

So where the French, and Japan, on the other hand, fully exploited China and the Korean Peninsula for quite some time until 1945, the Spaniards, Portuguese, Russians, and Americans exploited their "sphere of influence" rather than genuinely integrating parts of East Asia, China, South Asia, and Central Asia as they were not in their interests.

Rather, British in India and Japanese developed an understanding and signed an agreement not to interfere in their respective and exploitive spheres of influence in South and East Asia until the early 1920s. Trade was also discouraged between British India and Japan during colonialization.

---

[12] Ahmad Rashid Malik, Mutually Beneficial CPEC, *The Nation* (*Islamabad*), 2 May 2016.
[13] Board of Investment, Country-wise FDI flow (2016). Available at http://boi.gov.pk/ ForeignInvestmentinPakistan. aspx (accessed on 29 September 2016).

After the end of colonialization by the 1940s, Asian nation-states mainly remained busy with the nation-building processes. Little effort was paid on the regional trade integration. The Association of South East Asian Nations (ASEAN) emerged as the main locomotive of the intra-ASEAN trade integration by the late 1960s.

The incorporation of China into the ASEAN process in 1995 was a significant milestone in the promotion of regional trade connectivity. China emerged as the major trading partner of a number of ASEAN members. The country also emerged as the source of in-bound and out-bound investment. This flourished regional trade and investment between ASEAN and China. In the ASEAN–China trade nourishment, these were ASEAN members who played the leading role in bringing China into ASEAN's hold.

The two-decade long ASEAN–China promising relations have resulted in China's B&R Initiative as espoused by President Xi Jinping during his visit to Jarkarta in October 2013. The purpose was the continuity of trade relations as developed by ASEAN and China by making the canvas much broader by incorporating, inter alia, East Asia, South Asia, West Asia, as well as the African and European continents.

This was the Chinese thinking in contrast to imperialist and colonialist thinking. China does not promote either exploitation or imperialism but a cooperative relationship. It would like to share the development experience across the whole world. China has been offering the world's ever largest trade connectivity by integrating the whole Asian continent as well as giving benefits to nearby Africa and Europe.

China conducts around US$ 5 trillion merchandise trade via the Indian and the Pacific Oceans. The route is pretty long, up to 16,000 km. There are some choke points at the Straits of Malacca and the South China Sea. If some trade was diverted to land route through Pakistan, it would be safer as well as economical. The route from Gawader to Kashgar is approximately 2,500 km. The oil pipeline would be safer and quicker.

Given this regional context of the B&R Initiative's regional connectivity in the Indian Ocean and South China Sea, the CPEC, in fact, promotes Pakistan's regional trade by introducing new trading routes and by modernizing the old trading routes. The CPEC is not just a name of a road or a route but a system of communications network to connect all parts of Pakistan and the region. New infrastructure of roads and carriages are under construction in Baluchistan, Sindh, Punjab, Khyber Pakhtunkhwa, Azad Kashmir, and Gilgit–Baltistan. This would transform Pakistan into the "most physical infrastructural developed country" in Asia on modern telecommunication lines.

Provinces and major cities will be connected by high-speed limited access highways, motorways, bridges, tunnels, and railway tracks. China plans to ply high-speed railways in Pakistan. Chinese high-speed railways run between 200 and 350 km/h speed. This will change the outdated railway system of Pakistan that will be re-built on modern patterns.

China is a global leader in high-speed railways far ahead of Japan, United States, Germany, etc. At the moment, China's railway industry is engaged in infrastructure negotiations with at least 30 countries. China's high-speed railways bidding is much lower than developed countries.

In past 12 years, China has built 16,000 km of high-speed tracks within its borders — longer than the rest of the world's network combined. China has been building high-speed railways in Indonesia and Russia and it has been investing in high-speed railway in California. China outlawed Japan in Indonesian high-speed railway's bid this year.

If a 200 km/h moderate bullet train runs between Karachi–Peshawar, it could reach in 9 h, and between Islamabad–Lahore, 1 h 15 min. Days long distances between all cities will be reduced. This will be a miracle in rail transportation in Pakistan with Chinese rail projects under the CPEC. An intra-city Orange Line Metro train construction is already underway in Lahore.

China will invest U\$18 billion in a 200 km long tunnel at Babusar that will ensure year-round rail service, something that will revolutionize interregional travel and freight carriage.[14] An optic fiber cable has been planned from Kashgar to Rawalpindi to provide faster and safer internet services to Pakistan from China.

All type of industries will be built. The CPEC would turn Pakistan into a knowledge-based corridor and develop into a "truly Asian tiger" exporting hub economy meeting the growing demands of China and Central Asia.

---

[14] S. H. Sering, China's rise is a source of optimism for many in Pakistan, The American Bazaar (Germantown) (2013). Available at https://www.americanbazaaronline.com/2013/11/03/pakistan-chinas-soft-power-gilgit-baltistan/ (accessed on 28 September 2016).

10.5 Future Prospects

China is the only country among all friendly countries of Pakistan that qualifies to be the most trusted and true friend in all circumstances. Both are developing countries and China teaches Pakistan how to build a sustainable economy for a large population and under lesser resources. The CPEC is a shining example of the South–South cooperation. Pakistan is lucky to have China on its border. It is a matter of pride and jubilation. For Pakistanis, China has a soft image and a sustainable economy and they are striving hard to learn from China. The CPEC is bringing about an economic miracle on the Indus River similar to the miracle that happened in Japan after 1945, on the Han River in Korea, miracle that happened to ASEAN in the 1980s, and the miracle that happened on the Yellow River in China.[15] Analysts are of the opinion that this is the time for the Indus River miracle. The CPEC is greatly transforming the economy of Pakistan. The CPEC is also a knowledge corridor to educate people and to invest in science and technology. China is a now a popular destination for young Pakistani students learning sciences and technologies in various fields. The CPEC would bring about a civilizational transformation in the wider Asian Continent with Pakistan as the focal point. The CPEC is Pakistan's shared future destiny not only with China but with the entire Asian countries. The CPEC symbolizes iron friendship between Pakistan and China. The CPEC has created a soft image between the two countries. The CPEC is the most powerful tool to illuminate the Pakistan–China friendship at this point in time by leaders, diplomats, and scholars. The bright future of Pakistan's economy would be greatly linked with the CPEC and China's global economy. This would greatly help convert Pakistan economy along modern completive patterns. In a nutshell, the CPEC is actually an "economic game changer" of Pakistan's trade, regional road connectivity, and the economy.

---

[15] A. R. Malik, A miracle on the Indus River, *The Diplomat* (*Tokyo*), 7 December 2015.

CHAPTER 11

The Belt and Road Initiative and Afghanistan's Role in Multifield Cooperation with Other Powers*

Sayed Mahdi Munadi

Center for Strategic Studies, Ministry of Foreign Affairs,
Afghanistan

11.1 Introduction

This chapter focuses on three issues: first, the importance of Afghanistan economically for the economic corridors of regional and beyond regional actors; second, the importance of the Belt and Road Initiative (B&R) and other corridors; third, Afghanistan's capability of facilitating and connecting collaboration in the economic corridors.

11.2 Importance of Afghanistan Geoeconomically for the Economic Corridors of Regional and Beyond Regional Actors

Afghanistan is a land transit hub for the three economic initiatives. There are many economic initiatives which are potentially connecting

---

*The chapter does not officially reflect the policy of Afghanistan, it is just an academic approach.

with Afghanistan. The most important goal of these initiatives is to liberate trade and energy between South, West, Central Asia. Afghanistan connects these three important regions with these initiatives.

In these initiatives, we have four issues that cover the region.

- **Energy**
  (1) TAPI GAS Pipeline
  (2) CASA-1000
  (3) TAP-500 KV
  (4) Afghanistan–Tajikistan Gas Pipeline

- **Transport Networks**
  (1) Joining the B&R Initiative
  (2) Lapis Lazuli, Trade and Transport Route Agreement
  (3) International Transport and Transit Corridor (Chabahar Agreement)
  (4) Five-Nation Railway Corridor
  (5) Afghanistan Rail Network
  (6) Trans-Hindukush Road Connectivity Project

- **Transit Facilitation**
  (1) APTTA Implementation
  (2) CBTA and TIR Convention
  (3) Special Economic Zones/Multimodal Transport and Logistic Facilities
  (4) Regional Customs and Border Management Cooperation

- **Communications**
  (1) Digital Silk Road
  (2) B2B and Labor Support
  (3) Enhancing Regional B2B Partnership
  (4) Afghanistan–Kyrgyz Republic–Tajikistan AGRO Food Industry Development
  (5) Labor Exchange and Remittance.

With this understanding, Afghanistan can be considered a good stage for multifield cooperation with other powers of these three regions.

The Silk Road has been proposed by different powers in our region as follows:

- The first one is the B&R Initiative in which Afghanistan is directly or indirectly included.
- The second one is the Silk Road Initiative, which involves Kazakhstan, Azerbaijan, Georgia, and Turkey.
- The third one is the India–Iran corridor from Chabahar to Central Asia.
- The fourth is the new Silk Road Initiative supported by the US.
- The fifth one is the Turkey corridor which was modeled with the Silk Road project; in addition, the project about that train is included in this issue.

11.3 Importance of the B&R Initiative and Afghanistan

There are more than three Silk Roads going from Central Asia with a little change; the first is the Northern Distribution Network which is considered as a US network, however, it is not met yet; the second one is the B&R Initiative; the third one is Lapiz Lazuli, which is proposed by Afghanistan and Turkey. All these roads are somehow passing the same way but from different actors.

This looks as if we do not facilitate communication between these three ways, so we have got multiple ways without cooperation. If they support each other, the result is clear that we will have a more integrated region.

So far, all land lock countries need to develop through connecting with trade and transit corridors while Afghanistan can enjoy improvement being part of the B&R Initiative. The B&R Initiative as an opportunity for Afghanistan has a strong role for development via trade and transit. Along with the implementation of the B&R Initiative, Afghanistan and China both signed an MOU on 16 May 2016. It seems beyond this MOU, there is no action plan for the development of these huge initiatives. This chapter recommends an action plan for the development of the B&R Initiative between Afghanistan and China which can help us to improve the implementation. A clear task and action plan with specific timetable between both states and states along the B&R Initiative will facilitate expected results in a specific time.

Along the concept of the B&R Initiative, an important event for Afghanistan trade and transit was held on 7 September 2016 in the north of Afghanistan. We received the first train from China filled with Chinese products. It was very important for Afghanistan and all media in Afghanistan to cover this arrival as an important event in the history of this country to have received a direct train from China with whom we can have direct economic relation. Considering the route and ways of this train, it did not come from the original way of the B&R Initiative. It came from a different way than that proposed by the B&R Initiative which was a bit different, which confused people. For example, this event was very important for Afghanistan and people were very happy. Furthermore, this example and other elements lack adequate infrastructures, so we cannot just have unique or one B&R Initiative from Central Asia. We might have a different route along the economic initiatives in Central Asia. This might be considered as a shortage, but it is one of the important sources of strength in this diverse region.

Considering the above-mentioned aspects, it is necessary to emphasize that there should be an illustrative study on the possibility of cooperative relations between all stakeholders' economic initiatives in Central Asia. Looking at all the regional initiatives in Central Asia proposed by different stakeholders, we find a lot of overlapping. The Chinese B&R Initiative, the US initiative, Turkey, Indian, and Iranian Initiatives are all looking to meet their goals and facilitate cooperation through economic initiatives with states along their initiatives. A comprehensive and illustrative study for cooperation beyond states along each initiative with stakeholders may help to reach the initiative at lower price. Additionally, this cooperation reduces the competition among stakeholders due to gains from the economic initiatives. Afghanistan can play an important role in this study to facilitate coordination and cooperation between all economic projects with the concept of the Silk Road.

11.4 Afghanistan and its Capability in Facilitating Connection and Collaboration between Economic-Trade Corridors

Since 2001, Afghanistan allocates a huge amount of money toward its security, and gaining political international support. It is necessary to share some lessons learnt from mistakes which international actors made in Afghanistan and we need not repeat them.

- First, international coalition made Afghanistan more economically dependent on foreign aid, especially when there was no stable structure to use the aid affectively. They should have invested instead of giving aid.
- Second, we have defeated terrorism just militarily; we have missed an opportunity to facilitate a good economy and stability so as to not let the jobless people join terrorist groups.
- Third, we trusted nations with double standard policy, especially Pakistan.
- Fourth, it is not enough just to lean on international actors or beyond actors, we need regional cooperation. It is not possible to meet our goals just with regional actors; in contrast, we need international and beyond regional actors involved. Afghanistan can be a good stage, facilitating connectivity among West Central and South Asia, as well coordination and cooperation with the US concept of Silk Road.

We recommend technical research on combining the B&R Initiative with other economic initiatives in South, West, and Central Asia.

Plural understanding in this conference and different approaches of stakeholders in this region shows that the B&R Initiative does not mean to have one specific way or route toward development. There should be many routes and belts in our region. Finally, the B&R Initiative cannot be a pure economic initiative; rather, it should be an economic, political and security initiative. Through a cumulative approach of the B&R Initiative we can have economic means to tackle insecurity.

CHAPTER 12

Sri Lanka's Perspective on the Belt and Road Initiative

Janaka Wijayasiri

Institute of Policy Studies, Colombo, Sri Lanka

Before I speak on the Belt and Road (B&R) Initiative from Sri Lanka's perspective, I thought it would be good to give a background on the bilateral relations between Sri Lanka and China. In fact, the bilateral relations between Sri Lanka and China span centuries and is a multi-faceted relationship, as it has been outlined in a statement made by the Chinese Premier during the visit of the Sri Lankan Prime Minister to China earlier. He stated that both countries share the view that China and Sri Lanka are good friends who have been through the test of time and no matter what changes take place in the international landscape or in our domestic environment, our friendship and cooperation will always move forward.

Modern day relationship between China and Sri Lanka was established back in 1952 with the signing of a Rubber and Rice pact, which was subsequently followed by establishing diplomatic relations in 1957. More recently in 2014, Sri Lanka and China have elevated their relationship to a strategic economic partnership covering trade, economy, infrastructure development, science and technology, education and culture.

Over the years, China has made important contributions to Sri Lanka's economic and social development and has extended preferential loans and donations to the country, as well as constructed a number of megaprojects in the country including the ports, airports, highways, power plants, etc. You could see a number of landmarks in Colombo which have been donated by China, such as the Convention Center, the Supreme Court Complex, and also more recently a Cultural Center.

China extended support in the health sector in order to fight chronic kidney disease in Sri Lanka. China has also extended traineeships and scholarships toward building Sri Lanka's human resources.

In terms of bilateral trade between China and Sri Lanka, trade has expanded tremendously over the last five years. In fact, it has expanded at a much greater pace than Sri Lanka's trade with the rest of the world. Consequently, China has emerged as Sri Lanka's second largest trading partner and also an important source of import. In fact, China figures as the second largest source of imports into Sri Lanka. In terms of exports, China is the fifth largest export market after the US, UK, Germany, and Italy.

China has also emerged as an important foreign direct investor to the country over the last couple of years, and more recently China has become an important source of tourists to the country — in fact, becoming the second largest source of tourists to Sri Lanka. This has been facilitated by more air connectivity between Colombo and a number of destinations in China.

Speaking of the B&R Initiative, Sri Lanka has recognized the importance of the initiative and has pledged support toward it given that it coincides with Sri Lanka's own vision of establishing itself as a hub in the Indian Ocean. In this respect, Sri Lanka can play a very important role in the Maritime Silk Road, given its strategic location in the Indian Ocean. In fact, Sri Lanka has played this role in the past. In the ancient Silk Road, it has been an important entreport for exchange of goods in the Indian Ocean by connecting Asia with Africa and the rest of South Asia. Given Sri Lanka's strategic location and combined with its historical involvement in maritime cooperation makes Sri Lanka an important strategic partner in the maritime Silk Road.

As mentioned, China over the recent past has extended a huge support toward building infrastructure in the country in terms of highways, ports, airports as well as providing funds to modernize the southern container terminal in Colombo. Work has also recommenced on Sri Lanka's largest FDI project to date, the Colombo Port City project, which aims to expand the development space of Colombo city and stimulate investments and employment. This initiative, the Colombo Port City, which is now called the Financial City, will be an important stop in the Maritime Silk Road and will help to strengthen Sri Lanka's position as a hub in the Indian Ocean.

Other activities, which China will undertake in Sri Lanka in connection with the B&R Initiatives, include setting up of the industrial zone in the south of the country.

The B&R Initiative has five major objectives, which include policy coordination, connectivity, unimpeded trade, financial integration, and people-to-people contact. With regard to connectivity, this has been met by China investing in a number of megaprojects in Sri Lanka to develop the connectivity of Sri Lanka with the rest of the world.

With regard to trade, China and Sri Lanka negotiated a free trade agreement, which was signed in the middle of 2017.

With regard to financial integration, which is the other objective of the B&R Initiative, Sri Lanka is already a member of AIIB.

With regard to people-to-people exchange, there has obviously been a number of cultural and academy exchanges between China and Sri Lanka over the years, as well as influx of Chinese tourists into Sri Lanka. This has obviously gone toward meeting the objective of furthering people-to-people bond.

When it comes to challenges in terms of implementation, this initiative has raised concern over China's intentions given the ambitions of the plan due to a number of factors. One is because of the deficit in trust/lack of trust, and also competition among the super powers and emerging powers in the region. Therefore, the success of this initiative will be largely governed by geopolitical factors and how they are going to play out. Building trust will be an important means to address this issue. In this respect, Sri Lanka can play an important role in building this trust and gaining this trust given that Sri Lanka has cordial and good relations with all neighbors in South Asia. Sri Lanka could provide the necessary platform for China to connect with the other countries in the Indian Ocean and thereby cement its relationship, and dispel any concern with regard to the B&R Initiative.

In terms of other challenges, from the perspective of Sri Lanka, there should be much more consideration given to the lending standards. In the case of Sri Lanka, this has been lacking. This could impede the progress of the B&R Initiative, if monies are put into unfeasible projects which have no economic return.

Also, so far, much of the effort in Sri Lanka has been concentrated toward building connectivity and a lot of money has been invested in infrastructure development. But, the other four areas of the B&R Initiative have received less prominence in the case of Sri Lanka.

Moreover, there is little awareness in Sri Lanka of this important initiative beyond think tanks and policy circles. There should be more awareness of this initiative among the general public because people at large play an equally important role in this initiative.

Another concern has been the lack of detailed plan, which makes it difficult for countries to assess the full implications and the long-term benefits for the country concerned. So, from the perspective of Sri Lanka, it will benefit if there is much more participation or information with regard to detailed future plans of the B&R Initiative, so that we could absorb the initiative and make better use of initiative in the years to come and mutually benefit from it.

CHAPTER 13

The Belt and Road Initiative: The Bangladesh Context

Kazi Ali Toufique

Bangladesh Institute of Development Studies,
Dhaka, Bangladesh

13.1 Change in Bangladesh Economy

When Bangladesh became independent in 1970, there was a book written by two economists, Faaland and Parkinson. They said that Bangladesh is a test case of development, which means that we have very few land, backward technology, and too many people. They argued that if Bangladesh develops, then it will be a test case that with such an adverse condition, a country can develop or at least move forward.

We have gone through a big transformation of the economy from 1980 to 2014. As shown in Figures 13.1 and 13.2, the agricultural sector has declined in terms of its contribution to GDP. It has gone down from 33% to now merely 15–16%. It should be less by now (Figures 13.1–13.4). There is a structural transformation where the manufacturing sector is growing fast, now occupying around 25–26% of the GDP.

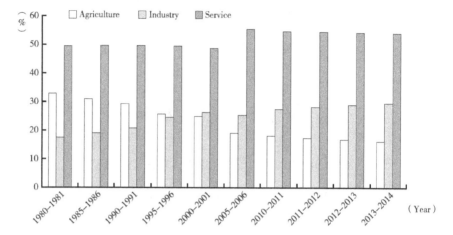

Figure 13.1: Structural Transformation of the Bangladesh Economy (1981–2014).
Source: MOF (2014).

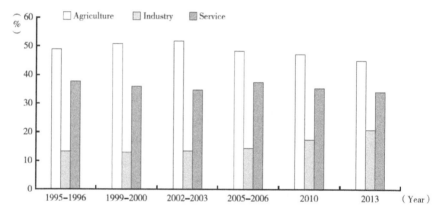

Figure 13.2: Structure of Employment in Bangladesh 1996–2013.
Source: Labor Force Surveys (various issues).

13.2 Current Constraints of Bangladesh Economy

It has the similar reflection in the employment situation where agriculture is still a dominant source of employment. About half of the population is involved in agriculture. But you see from the last few years, particularly from 2005 onwards, industrial employment, manufacturing employment as a proportion of total employment is growing reasonably fast.

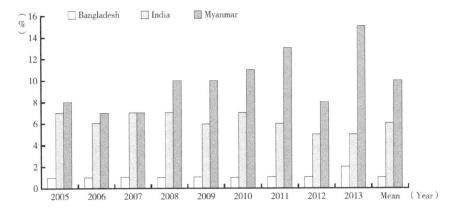

Figure 13.3: Chinese Imports from BCIM Countries.
Source: Morck and Yeung (2016).

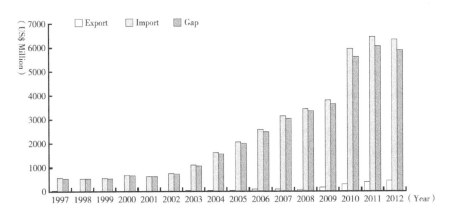

Figure 13.4: Massive Trade Gap between Bangladesh and China.
Source: Bangladesh Chambers of Commerce and Industries (BCCI).

Rodrik has a concept of de-industrialization hypothesis. He says that the developing countries now maximize their manufacturing employment at the lower level of per capita income. In the US and Europe, they maximized manufacturing employment when their per capita income was quite high, which means an average person could get a decent job from working in factories.

This thing does not happen. If you look at from 2006 onwards, employment in the manufacturing sector is increasing. One key reason is the big role played by the Readymade Garments (RMG) factor; we export garment products to the outside world. It grows very fast; though we are having problems over the last 4 or 5 years, our exports are still increasing. That keeps us still having a higher per capita income and higher manufacturing employment.

Wages as a consequence are increasing, and manufacturing wages are the highest. Poverty has declined sharply. In 1991, national poverty was about 55%. If you look at 2010 it has come down to about 33%. We have a projection for 2015, it has gone down further. It should be around 24–25%. We strongly believe that by 2030 we can meet the first goal of SDG that there will be no extreme poverty in Bangladesh at that time, which is very possible. This way, things are changing particularly in the rural area.

Our openness to the global economy has been increasing fast. 50% of our GDP is traded. The weaker part that we have is the tax–GDP ratio which is pretty low.

Bangladesh has been able to maintain a 6% GDP growth rate from the 1990s onwards. The recent forecast is around 6.8% GDP growth rate. The problem here is the investment rate. We are investing around 30% of our national product. But what happened was that private investment from 2012 to 2014 did not pick up.

13.3 Linking Bangladesh Economy with the B&R Initiative Context of BCIM

The government is trying to increase government investment. But somehow the private investment is not responding to this government investment. The big thing we are discussing now in Bangladesh for the last five years or so is that the private investment is not responding to government incentives.

Why is this important? It is so because the government has a plan, which is called Vision 2021, and wants to grow by 10% in 2021 which is our 50th year of independence. That is a very important year for us. So, we need huge investment but that is not forthcoming. We are still stuck below 7% growth rate. We are not able to go above 7% rate. We are very close to 7%. We cannot take it over 7%.

According to the World Bank, Bangladesh needs around 100 billion dollars of investment in infrastructure over the next 10 years. So, the government has planned large-scale infrastructure projects, deep sea ports, elevated expressways, power plants. Some are work in progress, and some are still under negotiation.

In this regard, the Chinese investment is considered to be very important, and for that reason in Chittagong, which is a port city in the south, two special economic zones are reserved for Chinese investment. If you look at Chinese investment commitment, between 2002 and 2009, it was around 300 million. Between 2010 and 2016, it was not even 1 billion, it was 900 million, or something like that. Now, the commitment from 2017 to 2021 is expected to be 23 billion.

Most of us have trade imbalances with China. We have massive trade imbalance with China, but in 2012 and 2013, it has become slightly better. Figure 13.4 shows that there is scope for increasing investment opportunities within the BCIM region. About 10% of Myanmar exports are actually imported by China. If you look at India, it is around 6%; if you look at Bangladesh, it is around 2%.

If you look at the trend, and if you compare India with China, for example, between 2005 and 2013, Indian exports to China actually declined. Indian exports to China as a percentage of imports of China declined from 6% to 5%. Exports have increased for Myanmar, export also increased for Bangladesh. Bangladesh is exporting more between 2005 and 2013 to China, which indicates there is room for increasing trade among these four countries.

The trade gap between Bangladesh and China in 2011 and 2012 has slightly improved.

In conclusion, Bangladesh economy is growing fast but more investment is required. There is huge demand for infrastructure investment in Bangladesh in the next few years, because for Vision 2021, we need investment and the economy has to grow around 9–10% per annum.

Regional cooperation among BCIM countries can boost investment and trade. There are many social indicators where Bangladesh has excelled over other South Asian countries. In order to take Bangladesh toward the next stage of the Belt and Road (B&R) Initiative, it has a strong role to play to help achieve a higher growth rate.

CHAPTER 14

The Evolution of Turkish–Chinese Trade Relations, 1990–2014

Dürdane Siirin Saracoglu

Department of Economics, Middle East Technical University, Ankara, Turkey

14.1 Introduction

The trade balance between Turkey and People's Republic of China (PRC) has been steadily deteriorating against Turkey since the early 1990s, when trade relations between these two countries started to gain momentum. In this study, the sources of this ongoing imbalance and the resulting effects on the Turkish economy are examined from different perspectives, namely the sectoral concentration of trade and the intra-industry trade (IIT). According to the findings, ever since the trade relations picked up between these two countries, imports from PRC into Turkey have always been more diversified than exports from Turkey into PRC, and since the mid-2000s, they have exhibited diversity particularly in mid-high and high-technology manufacturing sectors. Based on our results, although it may be difficult to correct the large trade balance between Turkey and PRC in favor of Turkey, higher diversification of exports to PRC and a shift toward manufacturing of higher value-added products appear to be essential.

Turkey, at the westernmost end, and China, at the easternmost end of the Asian continent, are two states with deep-rooted historical and cultural ties. Historically, before the emigration of the Turks from Central Asia into Anatolia, Turkish and Chinese people interacted frequently and these interactions date back to Han Dynasty (206 BC–220 AD) and the Great Hun Empire (established 220 BC), which is one of the first Turkic states. During the Tang Dynasty (618–907), the historical "Silk Road" had its brightest and most vibrant era, and during that time, close relations between the Gokturks in the north and the Chinese were flourishing. The "Silk Road" not only facilitated trade between the Chinese and the Turks but also enabled social and cultural interactions between these two societies.[1]

PRC–Republic of Turkey diplomatic relations were first established in 1971, but it was only in the 1980s when senior-level state visits started to take place between these two countries; however, relations were revived only by the end of 1990s when the Turkish governments felt the need to ameliorate the relations as the trade deficit between China and Turkey started to grow against Turkey.[2]

Since 2001, when the Turkish–Chinese trade volume surpassed US$ 1 billion, trade deficit against Turkey has been invariably increasing: in 2014, the trade deficit between Turkey and China has reached US$ 22 billion. In this study, we examine the development of trade relations between these two countries from the 1990s to the 2000s from different perspectives: sectoral concentration in trade analysis and the IIT analysis. We find that over the years, imports from China into Turkey remained more diversified than the exports to China from Turkey, and for the most part, the concentration in Turkish exports in the 1990s was in a mid-low technology-level sector, such as manufacture of basic iron and steel. However, in the 2000s, the concentration in Turkish exports to China has shifted to a mid-high technology-level sector, such as manufacture of man-made fibers. In the

---

[1] U. M. Sertel, *Türk Dış Politikasında Çin Halk Cumhuriyeti ile İşbirliği Olanaklarının Analizi (The Analysis of Cooperation Possibilities with the People's Republic of China in Turkish Foreign Policy)*, Unpublished Master's Thesis, Ankara, Atilim University (2008).
[2] C. Ergen, Can two ends of Asia Meet? An overview of contemporary Turkey–China relations, *East Asia* **32** (2015) 289–308.

early 1990s, imports from China mostly concentrated in low-technology-level sectors, but in the late 1990s and 2000s, this concentration is no longer valid; and in fact, imports from China have shifted toward high and mid-high technology-level sectors, but nevertheless a more diversified pattern of sectors exists in imports than in exports.

Examination of IIT in 71 sectors in Turkey shows that most of the IIT between Turkey and China occur in low-technology-level manufacturing: in food manufacturing, there is consistent IIT between these two countries since the mid-1990s. However, we do not observe such a pattern in any of the other industries or technology-level groups, indicating toward inter-industry trade between Turkey and China.

In Section 14.2, we summarize the Turkish–Chinese bilateral and trade relations for the period after 1990, when trade relations started to pick up pace. In Section 14.3, we evaluate Turkish–Chinese trade relations using concentration of trade indices and IIT indices at the sectoral level for the period after 1990. In Section 14.4, we conclude the study.

14.2 A General Outlook on Turkish–Chinese Trade Relations, 1990–2014

Diplomatic relations between the Republic of Turkey and the PRC had officially started in 1971. That said, the relations between the two countries followed a rather low profile until 1980. Although the first trade agreement between Turkey and China was signed in 1974, relations picked up pace only after May 1981 when the minister of trade realized the first high-level official visit from Turkey to China. Later in December 1981, the first economic, industrial, and technical cooperation agreement between these two countries was signed under the visit of the Foreign Minister from Turkey to China.

Turkish President Kenan Evren paid the first presidential visit to China from Turkey in December 1982. This visit was a milestone in bilateral relations between these two countries, as many senior-level visits between these two countries followed afterwards (see Footnote 1). After a slowdown in bilateral relations up until the end of 1990s, official senior-level visits between China and Turkey accelerated and intensified between

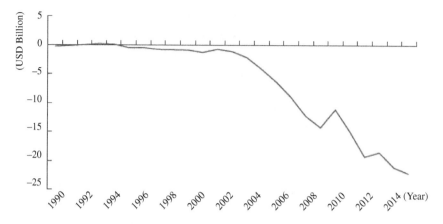

Figure 14.1: Turkey's Trade Balance with China, 1990–2014.

2000 and 2006, and the bilateral relations between these two countries, which are both current G20 members, have been growing quite rapidly in the recent periods. Nonetheless, Turkey and China still need to take certain major steps in political and economic areas toward a higher "strategic partnership."[3]

Trade relations between Turkey and China have been steadily progressing since the year 2001 when the trade volume between these two countries surpassed US$ 1 billion. However, starting at the same year with the accession of China to the World Trade Organization (WTO), the imbalance in bilateral trade against Turkey has been increasing more and more. In 2014, Turkey's and China's bilateral trade volume had reached US$ 28 billion: Turkey's exports to China were about US$ 3 billion, 1.8% of the country's total exports, while imports from China reached US$ 25 billion, 10.3% of Turkey's imports.[4] Currently, China is the third largest trading partner of Turkey after Germany and Russia.

As can be observed from Figure 14.1, Turkey's trade balance with China has been steadily worsening since the 1990s, particularly picking up pace after 2001, in 2014, Turkey's trade deficit with China had

---

[3] In October 2010, Turkey and China signed a "Strategic Partnership agreement" on trade, cultural and technical exchange, marine cooperation, among others.

[4] All trade-related data come from trade statistics of Turkish Statistical Institute (TurkSTAT).

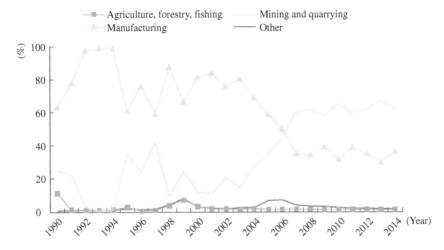

Figure 14.2: Sectoral Distribution of Turkish Exports to China, 1990–2014.

reached US$ 22 billion, while the country's overall trade deficit for that year was US$ 84 billion.

In Figure 14.2, we depict the sectoral distribution of Turkish exports to China for the period, 1990–2014. At the start of the 1990s, the prominent sector was manufacturing, with the manufacture of basic metals exports taking the lead. Up to 2003, basic metals remained as the most important export item with up to 48% of all exports in 2003, but toward the mid-2000s, export of non-ferrous metal ores (except uranium and thorium ores) and export of stone, sand and clay together picked up and reached 62% of all exports in 2013. In the 2000s, we can say that the focus of the exports from Turkey to China has shifted from "mid-low-technology" intermediate goods manufacturing to "raw materials".

Although we observe that Turkish exports to China have shifted from mid-low technology manufacturing to raw materials in the mid-2000s, within manufacturing exports, we also see a shift from mid-low to mid-high-technology intermediate goods, dominated by the manufacture of basic chemicals (Figure 14.3).

Exports of low-technology manufacturing, mostly food products (production, processing and preservation of meat, fish, fruit, vegetables, oils, and fats), fur, and spinning, weaving and finishing of textiles, became the second most important manufacturing export item, reaching 34% in 2013.

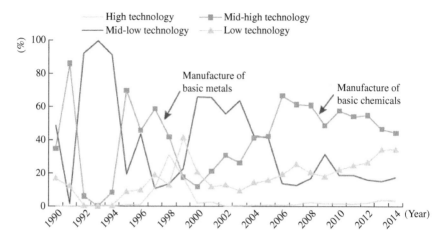

Figure 14.3: Technological Distribution of Turkey's Manufacturing Exports to China.

Nevertheless, we must recall that manufacturing exports to China fell down to about 35% of all exports to China in the mid-2000s, while raw materials exports gained dominance.

As for imports from China to Turkey, since the mid-1990s, almost 100% of all imports are in manufacturing. Over time, as Figure 14.4 depicts, we see some variation within manufacturing: in the 1990s, low-technology imports, mainly textile imports dominated, but in the early 2000s, we see a shift first toward high-technology manufacturing (reaching 33% of manufacturing exports in 2000), and in mid-2000s, import of mid-high-technology manufacturing gains importance and remains as the dominant import category since 2005, reaching 36% of all imports in 2014. Within the mid-high-technology manufacturing category, one cannot observe that one single sector highly dominates, rather, we see a high degree of diversification of imports in this category. That is, on average, each sector within this category makes up about 2% of all imports. Nevertheless, the largest share belongs to the manufacture of general-purpose machinery with 6.5% of all imports, and the second largest share belongs to manufacture of basic chemicals with 6% of all imports.

Although high-technology manufacturing remains as the second most important import category with 30% of all imports in 2014, individual sectors within this category show dominance over all the other

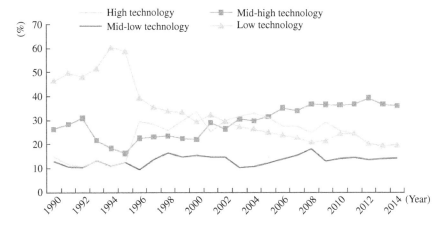

Figure 14.4: Technological Distribution of Chinese Manufacturing Imports to Turkey.

sectors: manufacture of television and radio transmitters and apparatus for line telephony and line telegraphy (ISIC code 332), and manufacture of office, accounting and computing machinery (ISIC code 300) makes up for 13% and 9% of all imports, respectively, in 2014.

The imbalance in the technological level of products imported from China and exported to China gives us an idea about the source of the large imbalance in trade at US$ 22 billion deficit against Turkey. Historically, in the last decades, Turkey has exported mainly raw materials and partly, mid-low and mid-high technology-level intermediate goods, and this pattern has not changed over the years. But Turkey's imports from China shifted from low-technology textiles to high-technology consumer goods in the 2000s, and to capital goods (general-purpose machinery) to some extent. In this sense, we can conclude that the imbalance in Turkey's and China's trade stems from the imbalance in the value-add of the goods traded.

14.3 An Assessment of Turkish–Chinese Trade Relations Under Different Approaches

14.3.1 *Sectoral Concentration Analysis*

In order to assess the sectoral concentration in Turkey's trade with China, we use two distinct measures: the Concentration Ratio (CR) and the

Gini–Hirschmann Index (GHI). The CR shows the share of k sectors (CRk) with the largest contribution to total (exports or imports with a partner country):

$$CR(K) = \left(\sum_{i=1}^{k} p_{it} \right) \times 100,$$

where $p_{it} = \frac{q_{it}}{q}$ denotes the share of sector i at year t in total exports or imports with a partner country.

Here, the selection of the number of sectors of concentration (k) is rather arbitrary, but nevertheless, this measure is widely used due to its ease of calculation. In our study, we use CR1 (share of the one sector with the highest contribution in total exports or imports) and CR4 (sum of shares of four sectors with the highest contribution in total exports or imports). In periodical bulletins on concentration in the manufacturing industry, the Turkish Statistical Institute (TurkSTAT) measures concentration ratios based on CR4. Accordingly, concentration ratios can be classified as follows[5]:

- 0–30: low-level concentration;
- 31–50: medium-level concentration;
- 51–70: high-level concentration;
- 71–100: very high-level concentration.

Data used for the concentration analysis are based on Turkish–Chinese trade data from TurkSTAT on 78 ISIC Rev.3, 3-digit-level sectors in agriculture, and mining and quarrying (12 sectors), manufacturing (59 sectors), and services (7 sectors), for the period, 1990–2014. Figures 14.5 and 14.6 depict the CR1 and CR4 ratios of the concentration in exports and imports, respectively.

---

[5]S. Doğan and S. S. Kaya, 2011. Gümrük Birliği Sonrasında (1996–2009) Türkiye'nin Avrupa Birliği ile Diş Ticareti'nin Ülke ve Fasil Bazli Yoğunlaşma Analizi. *Ekonometrive İstatistik*. 14, p. 18.

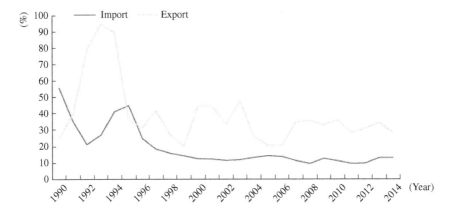

Figure 14.5: Concentration Ratio (CR1) of Turkey's Trade with China.

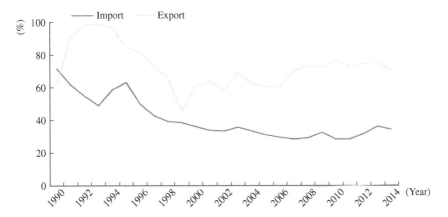

Figure 14.6: Concentration Ratio (CR4) of Turkey's Trade with China.

Another measure that is widely used in the calculation of concentration rate is the GHI[6]:

$$\text{GHI} = 100\sqrt{\sum_{i=1}^{n}\left(\frac{x_i}{X}\right)^2}.$$

---

[6]B. F. Massell, Export instability and economic structure, *The American Economic Review* **60**(4) (1970) 618–630; J. Love, Trade concentration and export instability, *Journal of Development Studies* **15**(33) (1979) 60–69.

Here, GHI denotes a country's trade (export or import) in sector i to a partner country, x_i and X denote the total trade (export or import) with a partner country, and n denotes the total number of sectors involved in trade. The smaller the index, the higher is the diversification in sectors in trade (export or import); as the index increases (close to 100), diversification diminishes, and concentration increases. This measure is relatively more reliable compared to the CR1 or CR4 measures, as it takes into account all the sectors involved in trade.

Both the CR1 and CR4 concentration measures and the GHI show that throughout the examination period, imports from China to Turkey have been relatively more diversified than the exports from Turkey to China. Especially, at the start of the 1990s, Turkish exports to China have been prominently concentrated in the manufacture of basic iron and steel (in 1993, the export volume of this sector to China was 94% of total exports to China Turkey) (see Figure 14.7). Although the export of basic iron and steel has somewhat subsided by mid-1990s, the exports from Turkey to China were still concentrated on raw materials and intermediate goods: mining of non-ferrous metal ores, manufacture of basic iron and steel; manufacture of basic chemicals, and manufacture of man-made fibers. Turkey's main import item from China was "crude petroleum and natural gas" from the beginning to mid-1990s. In the early 1990s, the sum of shares of four sectors with highest shares in exports was 90% on average,

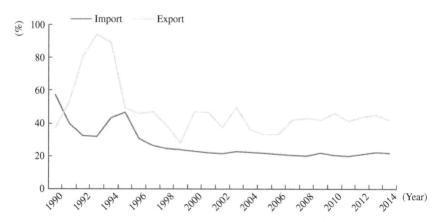

Figure 14.7:   GHI of Turkey's Trade with China, all Sectors.

whereas it was only 59% for imports. By mid-to-late 1990s, Turkey's exports to China still concentrated on raw materials and intermediate goods exports, most particularly mining of non-ferrous metal ores manufacture of basic iron and steel, and manufacture of man-made fibers, and the sum of shares of four sectors with highest shares in exports somewhat declined to about 70% on average, implying a slight increase in export diversification. By mid-1990s on the other hand, there has been a shift in imports from China toward textiles import: until 1999, the share of textiles imports from China has reached up to 40% of total imports from China, making textiles the most important import item from China to Turkey in mid-to late 1990s.

In the early 2000s, we still observe that raw materials and intermediate goods exports to China are dominant: in addition to manufacturing of basic chemicals, we still see that mining of non-ferrous metal ores and manufacture of basic iron and steel make up for the largest share in exports. But starting in 2002, we note that quarrying of stone, sand and clay becomes one of the important export sectors along with mining of non-ferrous metal ores and manufacture of basic iron and steel, starting with 7% of total exports to China in 2002, and quickly increasing to 29% in 2014, making it the sector with the highest contribution to exports to China from Turkey in 2014. After 2007, until 2014, we observe that mining of non-ferrous metal ores and quarrying exports still dominate, and the sum of these two make up to 60% of all exports to China; additionally, exports in manufacture of basic chemicals are still important. In summary, we can say that Turkish exports to China have concentrated heavily on raw materials and intermediate goods, mostly low-technology manufactured goods, and to some extent mid-high-technology manufactured goods, such as basic chemicals.

With the start of the 2000s, we observe that textiles imports from China to Turkey start to lose importance and with the textiles falling down to roughly 10% of total imports in 2003, imports from China begin to further diversify: high-technology manufacturing goods such as radio, television, and communication equipment and apparatus, office, accounting, and computing machinery, and electrical machinery and apparatus manufacturing imports gain significance in the 2000s and finally, the share of textiles imports in total imports fall to 2% by 2012.

In any case, imports from China to Turkey consistently remain more diversified than exports from Turkey to China, and within this diversification in imports, the sectors with the highest shares are the high-technology manufacturing sectors.

14.3.2 *Intra-Industry Trade Analysis*

IIT can be defined as the simultaneous export and import within the same industry.[7] In measuring the intra-industry rate of trade between Turkey and China, we use the Grubel–Lloyd (GL) index given as[8]

$$\mathrm{GL}_{it} = 1 \frac{\left|X_{it} - M_{it}\right|}{X_{it} + M_{it}}, \quad i = 1, \dots, n, \quad t = 1, \dots, T,$$

where X_{it} is the exports of Turkey to China in sector i at year t, M_{it} stands for the imports from China to Turkey in sector i at year t, and GL_{it} is the GL-index for the sector i at year t. The GL-index lies between 0 and 1, and the closer the index is to 1, the higher is the rate of IIT rate for sector i at year t. An index equal to or greater than 0.5 is an indicator of IIT for that specific industry, otherwise there is evidence of inter-industry trade.

A measure of IIT can be considered as an indicator of sectoral similarity of different countries: in order for two countries to be able to export goods of a specific sector to each other, they both have to be producing these goods.[9] In this sense, the GL-index for a particular sector will provide an indication of how similar that sector is between Turkey and China, especially in terms of the technological level. Several factors determine the extent of IIT,[10] such as (a) tastes and per capita

---

[7]R. Loertscher, and F. Wolter, Determinants of intra-industry trade: Among countries and across countries, *Weltwirtschaftslishes Archives* **116**(2) (1980) 280–293.

[8]H. G. Grubel and P. J. Lloyd, *Intra-Industry Trade: Theory and Measurement of International Trade in Differentiated Products* (Wiley, New York, 1975). D. Greenaway and C. Milner, On the measurement of intra-industry trade, *The Economic Journal* **93**(372) (1983) 900–908.

[9]M. Brülhart, An account of global intra-industry trade, 1962–2006, *The World Economy* **32**(3) (2009) 401–459.

[10]J. A. Stone and H.-H. Lee, Determinants of intra-industry trade: A longitudinal, cross—country analysis, *Weltwirtschaftslishes Archives* **131**(1) (1995) 67–85. Turkish Statistical

income (positive correlation with the extent of IIT); (b) scale economies (the larger the country is, the higher is the extent of IIT); (c) transaction costs (IIT is negatively correlated if the geographical distance between countries is larger); (d) openness (IIT is positively correlated with the country's trade orientation); and (e) trade imbalances (GL-index becomes smaller as the size of trade imbalances increases).

In calculating the GL-index for Turkey's IIT with China,[11] we use trade data from the TurkSTAT for the years, 1990–2014, covering 71 ISIC (Rev.3) 3-digit-level sectors in agriculture, and mining and quarrying (12 sectors) and manufacturing (59 sectors). For manufacturing, we categorize the sectors according to their technological levels: low technology (21 sectors), mid-low technology (12 sectors), mid-high technology (17 sectors), and high technology (9 sectors), based on OECD's classification of manufacturing industries into categories on the basis of R&D intensities.

In agriculture, farming of animals, forestry, and mining and quarrying, in the 1990s, we do not see any consistent IIT between Turkey and China. There is some sporadic IIT in the mining of non-ferrous metal ores sector, but this scattered IIT nevertheless ends by 2003. From 2001 to 2012, mining and quarrying, n.e.c.[12] sector consistently displays IIT between Turkey and China. From the 2000s up to 2014, again, some irregular IIT exists in fishing, and some in forestry sectors, but we can say that for the period examined, overall there is no permanent IIT between Turkey and China in agriculture, farming of animals, forestry, and mining and quarrying sectors from 1990s to the early 2000s.

Institute (TurkSTAT). Available at www.tuik.gov.tr.; D. P. Clark and D. L. Stanley, Determinants of intra-industry trade between developing countries and the United States, *Journal of Economic Development*, **24**(2) (1999) 79–95.

[11] Zhang and Zhou (2005) "calculate the IIT rates for China with Turkey (in aggregated sectors) and show that for the period, 1992–2001, although there is an increase over the period, these IIT rates remain much below the world average: for 1992–1994, it is 0.012, for 1995–1998, it is 0.084, for 1999–2001, it is 0.112. These rates are 0.31, 0.38, and 0.40 for the Chinese–World trade for the respective periods."

[12] This class includes mining and quarrying of various minerals and materials: abrasive materials, asbestos, siliceous fossil meals, natural graphite, steatite (talc), feldspar, etc.; gemstones, quartz, mica, etc.; natural asphalt, asphaltites and asphaltic rock; natural solid bitumen.

In certain low-technology manufacturing sectors, on the other hand, there is relatively more regular IIT between Turkey and China during 1990–2014. From 1995 to 1999, the production, processing, and preservation of meat, fish, fruit, vegetables, oils, and fats sector consistently exhibits IIT between Turkey and China, then in the early 2000s, there is an intermission, but again from 2006 to 2014, the IIT rates in this sector consistently remain above 0.5. The same observation can also be made for the manufacture of other food products[13] sector, in which, particularly in the 2000s, the IIT shows a continuous pattern. Other sectors in low-technology manufacturing also show some degree of IIT in the 2000s, such as manufacture of dairy products, and dressing and dyeing of fur and manufacture of articles of fur, but more sporadic compared to the food manufacturing.

In mid-low technology manufacturing, one cannot point to any consistent and regular IIT between Turkey and China for the whole period of 1990–2014. No sector in this technology category shows a persistent IIT between these two countries. In mid-high-technology manufacturing, on the other hand, manufacture of basic chemicals and manufacture of man-made fibers show IIT early on in the 1990s; however, this pattern does not continue in the late 1990s. Nevertheless, manufacture of basic chemicals in the late 2000s and manufacture of man-made fibers in the early 2000s showed some degree of regularity in terms of IIT. Lastly, the least number of occurrences of IIT can be observed in high-technology manufacturing. Only lately after 2010, we notice some regular IIT only in the manufacture of aircraft and space craft sector (though the volume of trade in this sector is minimal: in 2014, exports in this sector comprised 0.02% of all exports, and imports in this sector were only 0.003% of all imports).

These results from the IIT analysis show that on the sectoral basis, the IIT between Turkey and China since trading relations between these countries began in early 1990s has concentrated mainly in raw materials sector such as mining and quarrying, low-technology manufacturing sectors such as food manufacturing and manufacture of fur, and to some degree,

---

[13]This group consists of manufacture of bakery products, manufacture of sugar, manufacture of cocoa, chocolate and sugar confectionery, manufacture of macaroni, noodles, couscous and similar farinaceous products, manufacture of other food products, etc.

mid-high-technology manufacturing and intermediate goods sectors, such as basic chemicals and man-made fibers.[14] If one regards the IIT rate as the measure of the degree of similarity of sectors across countries, one can conclude that since the start of trade relations between Turkey and China, only these five sectors have shown similarity (in terms of use and level of technology, factors, etc). In all other sectors, we can say that inter-industry trade exists between Turkey and China.

14.4 Conclusion

In this study, we examined the Turkish–Chinese trade relations from 1990 to 2014 from two different points of view: first, we considered the degree of sectoral concentration of imports from China to Turkey and exports to China from Turkey, and then we explored the degree of IIT between Turkey and China in 71 sectors.

Looking at the progression of trade relations between these two countries, we first note the high and increasing trade deficit against Turkey: in 1990, Turkey's trade deficit with China was US$ 209 million, in 2000, it surpassed US$ 1 billion, and in 2014, it has reached US$ 22 billion (Turkey had a trade surplus with China only in years 1993 and 1994 by US$ 260 million and US$ 97 million, respectively). One of the main culprits of this imbalance was the unbalanced sectoral concentration in imports and exports: from 1990 onwards, through 2014, Turkish exports to China mainly concentrated in raw materials and intermediate goods, whereas imports to Turkey from China were relatively more diversified particularly in the 2000s, and these imports were increasingly more and more leaning toward high-technology and mid-high-technology manufacturing goods (in 2014, 67% of all imports from China were in mid-high and high-technology manufacturing); in fact, the most important import item with 13% of all imports in 2014 was a high-technology manufacturing product, i.e., manufacture of television and radio transmitters and apparatus for line telephony and line telegraphy.

---

[14]Our results agree with those of Deviren and Karata (2007), in which they find that for the period, 1995–2005, using SITC Rev.3 (3-digit) commodity classification, Turkish–Chinese IIT concentrates on food, live animals and chemicals.

Another source of imbalance in trade between Turkey and China is the existence of high-degree inter-industry trade, or the lack of IIT. High degree of inter-industry trade would point to similarities in sectors subject to trade; however, we see some degree of inter-industry trade between Turkey and China only in some low-technology (or low value-added) manufacturing sectors such as food manufacturing, and recently in raw materials sector, mining and quarrying. As we have seen in the concentration analysis, the sectors which are subject to exports, and sectors which are subject to imports are highly dissimilar in technology levels and thus are highly uneven in the value added.

The fact that since the 2000s, the bilateral trade between Turkey and China has turned into a unilateral trade mostly in high-technology consumer goods and mid-high-technology intermediate goods in favor of China points to a structural problem in Turkish manufacturing. In this respect, Turkish policymakers and Turkish manufacturing sector need to divert attention toward higher technology and higher value-added products and invest in R&D rather than concentrate on short-term profits. Independent of the strategies in restructuring the manufacturing sector, new strategies to reduce the trade deficit against Turkey need to be cultivated: in order to reduce the imbalance, projects involving investment in high-speed rail, nuclear power plant and mining sectors by Chinese companies need to be promoted[15] (Colakoglu 2013). One can say that as long as Ankara and Beijing are willing to make advances in developing new policy liaisons in order to solve the existing problems in a positive outlook, there is ample room for the Turkish–Chinese political and economic relations to grow.

Further Reading

N. V. Deviren and M. Karataş, Türkiye ile Çin Halk Cumhuriyeti Arasındaki Endüstri-içi Ticaret, *İktisat İşletme ve Finans.* **22**(250) (2007) 16–32.

J. A. Zhang and C. Zhou, Chinese bilateral intra-industry trade: A panel data study for 50 countries in the 1992–2001 period, *Review of World Economics*, **141**(3) (2005) 510–540.

---

[15]Çolakoğlu, Turkey–China relations: Rising partnership, *OrtadoğuAnaliz*, **5**(32) (2013) 32–45.

CHAPTER 15

The Belt and Road Initiative: The Future of Economic Relationship between China and Egypt

Amr I. A. Elatraby

Faculty of Commerce, Ain Shams University, Egypt

15.1 Background and Origin

The B&R Initiative was announced by the Chinese President Xi Jinping in 2013 as the Chinese development framework that will shape the Chinese economic development through the "going abroad strategy" in the upcoming decades. The initiative was initially divided into two economic initiatives, namely, the Silk Road Economic Belt (SREB) and the 21st Century Maritime Silk Road (MSR) and then these two initiatives were packaged and labeled the Belt and Road (B&R) Initiative.

Basically, the B&R Initiative is a concept that aims at increasing the links between the Asian, European and African continents. Such increased links would enable these countries to enhance trade flows and spur long-term regional economic growth and development, benefiting all those involved.[1]

---

[1] Pricewaterhouse Coopers (PwC), China's new silk route: The long and winding road, Growth Markets Centre (2016), p. 2.

That is, the B&R Initiative is a way for win–win cooperation that promotes common development and prosperity and a road toward peace and friendship by enhancing mutual understanding and trust, and strengthening all-round exchanges.

The SREB involves a land route running from inner China to Southern Europe (via the Netherlands), while the MSR is a sea route connecting the port of Shanghai ultimately with the end point of the land-based route in Venice, via India and Africa.

In this context, the B&R Initiative includes 65 partner countries in three continents (Asia, Europe, and Africa) and among these countries is Egypt with its historical friendship relations with China. In addition, the B&R Initiative could be considered a huge one as the involved countries represent about 55% of world Gross National Product (GNP), 70% of world population, and 75% of known energy reserves.[2]

15.2 Motivation and Objectives

The B&R Initiative was largely motivated by long-run economic and political drivers that aimed at facing the major obstacles that could hinder the sustainability of the Chinese economic and political success in the global arena.

On the one hand, although the Chinese economic growth record since the 1980s could be considered as a miracle, the Chinese economy has faced some challenges after the 2007 global financial crisis as the economic growth slowed largely with a smaller current account surplus in addition to over-investment in some sectors such as industry and construction.

Meanwhile, the Chinese growth experience has been accompanied with regional inequality as investments were concentrated mainly in the eastern and southern coastal provinces at the expense of the western and northern provinces. In other words, it can be said that the coastal

---

[2]I. I. Pop, Strengths and challenges of the "Belt and Road" initiative, Centre for Geopolitics and Security in Realism Studies (2016), p. 6.

provinces have benefited more from growth as such provinces were connected to the global economy through trade and investment.[3]

On the other hand, the B&R Initiative can be regarded as a political strategy that could develop geopolitical influence in international politics by enhancing the relationships with neighboring countries as well as extending the Chinese influence outside Asia by building strong political and economic ties with European and African partners.

The B&R Initiative has identified five major areas of interest for achieving its objectives. These areas are: policy coordination, facilities connectivity, unimpeded trade, financial integration, and people-to-people bond.

In reality, the B&R Initiative is more of a large multisectorial initiative. It seems to be a potentially huge collection of current, planned and future infrastructure projects, accompanied by bilateral and regional trade agreements as well as investment ties. Current and planned projects will focus on the development of a wide array of infrastructure projects, including ports, roads, railways, airports, power plants, oil and gas pipelines and refineries, and Free Trade Zones, as well as a supporting IT, telecom, and financial infrastructure.

Thus, it seems that the initiative will serve several economic and political objectives. Among these objectives are:

(1) Exporting overcapacity industries such as cement and steel;
(2) Increasing trade and investment ties with involved countries;
(3) Developing inland China to catch up with the more advanced coastal provinces;
(4) Securing energy for the Chinese provinces;
(5) Widening the international use of the Chinese domestic currency;
(6) Expanding the Chinese geopolitical influence outside Asia.

However, the B&R Initiative should not be viewed as serving the Chinese interests solely, it should be viewed as a multilateral initiative that

---

[3]D. Dollar, China's rise as a global and regional power: The AIIB and the "Belt and Road", *Journal of International Relations and Sustainable Development*, (4) (2015) 162–163.

aims at achieving the prosperity of the partner countries through building mutually beneficial trade and investment ties, providing the partner countries with the required infrastructure projects, and developing strong and friendly political relations. In this sense, the B&R Initiative could be considered as a movement toward more fair, adaptable, and friendly multilateral economic and political order.

Such mutually beneficial nature of the B&R Initiative is justified by "the three Nos" that have been emphasized by President Xi Jinping:

No interference in the internal affairs of other nations;
Does not seek to increase the so-called "sphere of influence"; and
Does not strive for hegemony or dominance.[4]

The achievement of the above-mentioned objectives will require huge funds that could be provided from multilateral financial institutions. In this regard, the funds would be provided through three newly founded institutions, which are as follows:

1. **Silk Road Infrastructure Fund:** It was launched in February 2014 with the aim of investing US$40 billion in the B&R Initiative Infrastructure projects. The fund is capitalized mainly by China's foreign exchange reserves and is intended to be managed like China's sovereign wealth fund.

2. **Asian Infrastructure Investment Bank:** Asian Infrastructure Investment Bank (AIIB) was founded in October 2014 and aspires to be a global development bank with a registered capital of US$ 100 billion, which would be invested in the B&R Initiative infrastructure projects.

3. **New Development Bank:** The New Development Bank (NDB) is a BRICS multilateral development bank established in July 2014 by Brazil, Russia, India, China, and South Africa (BRICS countries). The bank was seeded with US$ 50 billion initial capital with the

---

[4]Credit Lyonnais Securities Asia (CLSA), *One Belt, One Road: A Brilliant Plan*, Available at https://www.clsa.com/special/onebeltoneroad/.

intention to increase capital to US$ 100 billion. Each country will have one vote and no country will have veto power.

Moreover, the foundation of AIIB and NDB with their current regulations and terms justifies that the B&R Initiative aims at building a fair, adaptable, and non-bureaucratic multilateral development bank that will try to avoid the defects of the current dominating multilateral development banks such as the World Bank. In other words, it could be concluded that the B&R Initiative is a huge real step toward a fairer and friendly economic order.

15.3 The Relationship between China and MENA Countries[5]

China's thirst for energy has guided much of the country's Middle East policy, and Beijing seeks to maintain positive relations with all the countries in the region. As the Chinese economy grew, its oil imports also surged from US$ 664 million in 1980 to US$ 235.75 billion in 2011. China is today the world's largest oil importer. China will spend about US$ 500 billion on crude oil imports by 2020, while the share of the OPEC in Chinese imports will rise from 52% in 2005 to 66% in 2020.

China uses its large foreign currency reserves to acquire equity stakes in energy companies, with Chinese National Oil Companies (NOCs) purchasing $18 billion in overseas assets in 2011, including investments in the MENA region. To foster closer relations with Baghdad, Beijing forgave about 80% of Iraq's $8.5 billion debt to China in 2010 and has signed multibillion-dollar trade deals in the heavy industry, government, tourism, transportation sectors among others.

Focused on affordable consumer goods and services, such as construction and engineering, Chinese exports to the MENA region have been modest but steadily increased from 2.8% in 1994 to 5.8% in 2010.

Egypt's large population provides a consumer market for inexpensive Chinese products and the country's strategic assets can also further China's interests in the region. Egypt in return can offer China economic

---

[5]T. C. Liu, China's economic engagement in the Middle East and North Africa, FRIDE, Policy Brief, No. 173, January 2014.

and geopolitical influence in Africa and the Middle East. As a traditionally influential player in the Arab world, a closer relationship with Egypt could buy China political goodwill in the region, but may also facilitate practical benefits such as expedited access to the Suez Canal for Chinese commercial vessels and warships.

After France and Italy, China is Algeria's third largest source of imports. The Chinese economic footprint in Algeria is most pronounced in the infrastructure development sector. For example, Chinese firms built a large chunk of the 1,216 km East–West highway to link Algeria's divergent regions.

15.4 Future of Economic Relationship between China and Egypt

Egypt and China have been enjoying solid economic ties which date back to more than half a century. The volume of Egyptian exports into China has increased remarkably since 1994, particularly in the last few years. However, the year-on-year growth rate has been characterized by sharp fluctuations. China's exports into Egypt have been far greater than its imports from Egypt, resulting in a large trade surplus in favor of China (Figure 15.1).

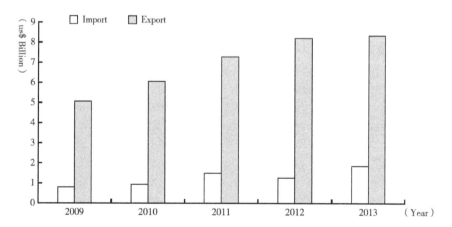

Figure 15.1: China–Egypt Bilateral Trade.

While the growing China–Egypt trade relationship is clear, the trade imbalance present since the 1980s has worsened significantly over time. This imbalance can partly be explained by each country's population size as a contributing factor toward Gross Domestic Product (GDP), and partly by the types of products being exported. Chinese exports to Egypt, while mass manufactured, are value added products, whereas China's imports from Egypt mainly consist of primary commodities and light industry products. The growth in Chinese exports to Egypt is, on the one hand, a realization of China's long-standing objective to develop export markets abroad (where Egypt is currently China's largest export market in Northern Africa) and, on the other hand, is the symbol of China's growing trade surplus worldwide. Consequently, Egypt may become more dependent on China as an export market than vice versa over the long term. Without determined corrective action, the trade imbalance seems to set to worsen and distort further.

15.5 Egypt's Overall Trade Balance

Both the Egyptian and the Chinese governments turned to economic and technological zone in Suez (SEZs), and their variants when they firmly decided to open up their economies in order to develop. The preferential policies offered to companies in Egypt SEZs are almost identical to China's, which leads to the conclusion that Egypt has, indeed, attempted to copy the Chinese model. While these policies have attracted FDI, some of them undermine Egypt's domestic production, while clearly working in favor of China's export policy.

The bilateral dialogue between China and Egypt should concern the following:

(1) Establishing national organization of public diplomacy in both countries that gathers in its membership all who are interested and concerned with the Egyptian Chinese affairs.
(2) Presenting a unified vision, its message is to meet the needs of the Egyptian–Chinese relations through knowledge exchange between the two people to face the challenges and increase the developmental links.

(3) Presenting activation mechanisms to this organization based on presenting the executive list to coordinate with official ones through the following terms:

   (3.1) The official organizations provide all the guarantees that achieve the message of the national organization and remove the complicated bureaucratic procedures of this organization.

   (3.2) Enhance the constructivist structure of the National Foundation by forming a strategic work group to look into how the Egyptian Chinese relations with its different dimensions should be.

   (3.3) Develop the management of translation and publication of the Egyptian and Chinese compositions and writings; also, work on exchange of such publications between the two cultures which would lead to strengthening the bond between these people.

Further Reading

E. Scott, China goes global in Egypt: A special economic zone in Suez, Centre for Chines Studies, Discussion Paper No. 2 (213).

E. Scott, China–Egypt trade and investment ties: Seeking a better balance, Centre for Chines Studies, Policy Briefing (2015).

A. R. Abu-Hatab, A. Nada, Shoumann and H. Xuexi, Exploring Egypt-China bilateral trade: Dynamics and prospects, *Journal of Economic Studies*, **39**(3) (2012) 214–326.

S. A. S. Farrag, Egyptian-Chinese relations: Opportunities and risks for Egypt (2016).

Part 3

The Belt and Road Initiative and Construction of "Soft Power"

CHAPTER 16

Soft Power: A Flexible Tool for Cooperation

Innara A. Guseynova

Moscow State Linguistic University, Moscow, Russia

Numerous researchers studying the current situation in international humanitarian area rightly point out/observe three tendencies: (1) servile — aimed at the destruction of the system of traditional/basic values shared by all the members of etnosocium/ethnic societies; (2) humanistic/ humanitarian — oriented at solving global environmental and social disasters; (3) cultural heritage value preservation — aimed at maintenance of national cultural originality and historical past of a concrete country.

The above-mentioned tendencies require different implementation strategies. For example, the servile approach to traditional/basic values includes intensive employment of negative stereotypes, which destroy a positive country's image, terminate its achievements and humiliate the whole nation consciousness. This could find expression in various stereotypes broadcast by mass media — newspapers, magazines, internet publications, television, and radio. The advocates/supporters of the servile school mainly rely on political and ethnic stereotypes. Certain features, expressed by lexical units, meaning aggressor, enemy, spy and such, are attributed to entire countries/nations. It is not infrequent that they make use of realia associated with governmental institutions and law enforcement agencies, which have a conceptual meaning for the foreign recipient. The servile tendencies are carried out in mass media by means of excessive use of borrowings. The following abstract from a popular intellectual edition, criticizing the phenomenon, would be appropriate here:

> "It is not more than 300 m to the Kremlin, the Roman alphabet is triumphant: a shopping center "Luxury Nikol's kaya Plaza"; fashion brands; beauty parlor "Persona"; a fitness-club "Republika"; a show-room "Audi City Moscow."[1]

There is no doubt these are indications of globalization, demonstrating the erasure of national and cultural borders, convergence of different people imposed though by exclusively economic reasons. Modern industries tend to promote and sell products abroad, to form brands — easily recognizable semiotic signs which strengthen the role of the country exporting the produce and services. Thus, the servile tendencies provide for secondary value system promotion, washing away traditional, basic values, like family, peace, labor, and others.

The second trend/tendency is represented most by mass pop-culture — cinema, television, and popular fiction. For the western-type mass culture, it is typical to show superheroes single-handedly rescuing the planet from the evil. Supporters of this approach rely on the biblical plots and sacred mythology. Apocalyptical motives are based on a fundamental human emotion — fear. It is a common knowledge that the fear of punishment and retribution makes people do good deeds and follow certain rules. In the light of the above-mentioned considerations, it is clear why the key role is given to various institutions, like church, governmental structures, who control social interaction/cooperation within the society and among representatives of various lingua-cultures. American feature-films, made in accordance with a cliché/commonplace pattern, are well known to the mass audience in the whole world.

The third tendency combines the cultural management strategies, including three factors: economic success, ideological cogency/convincingness,

---

[1] Л. Мазурова, Иностранный какрусский. — Литературная газета. — № 39 (6569), 5 – 11 октября 2016 г. — с. 18 (2016).

and cultural attractiveness of a country.[2] These factors also form the basis of "soft power" strategy, ensuring world domination in social and humanitarian areas. First of all, what is at issue is communication technology to establish partnership and cooperation with countries of different cultural phenotypes. Second, it is about developing the system of soft influence on all the parties of an international cultural dialogue, which could be achieved by means of demonstrating cultural and technological progress of a country in literature, arts, modern industrial technologies, innovations implemented, etc. Last but not least is the role of sports and other socially relevant practices. To sum it up, institutional interaction in a modern humanitarian space is carried out by means of employing various strategies. However, the "soft power" strategy, ensuring success in intercultural communication, is of key priority for intercivilizational dialogue.

Cross-cultural communication is regarded as a dialogue of individuals, who belong to different lingua-cultural communities. In the process of its realization, the participants of the interaction use different strategies. One of the strategies used in the modern discourse and which runs through the institutional communication, at the same time aimed to overcome negative stereotypes, is called "SOFT POWER".

The term "POWER" has several meanings and can be interpreted as "AUTHORITY", "FORCE", "INFLUENCE", etc. The ambiguity of this term lets us determine at least three components in the "SOFT POWER" strategy so far: "CULTURAL COMPONENT" (a system of basic values, shared by all the members of society); "IDEOLOGICAL COMPONENT" (a set of beliefs in different areas — from scientific knowledge to religion and common beliefs about socially accepted behavior); "FOREIGN-POLICY COMPONENT" (diplomacy in a broad sense). Cultural and ideological components represent the stable part of the "SOFT POWER" strategy, whereas the foreign-policy component is dynamic and versatile which helps us overcome negative stereotypes disseminated mostly by the mass media.

---

[2]В. Д. Агеева, Рольинструментов "мягкой силы" во внешней политике Российской Федерации в контексте глобализации. — Автореф. дисс. — Санкт-Петербург: СпбГУС. 3 (2016).

Accomplishing several functions, cross-cultural communication provides mutual understanding among members of different ethnic societies; the "SOFT POWER" strategy helps us overcome different stereotypes, including ethnic stereotypes, and promotes sociocultural interaction. In the context of cross-cultural communication, the "SOFT POWER" ensures the implementation of a mediatory/mediating function aimed at forming partnerships between people, who represent different cultures, which creates multipolar space in social and virtual realities.

Further Reading

В. Д. Агеева, Рольинструментов "мягкой силы" во внешней политике Российской Федерации в контексте глобализации. — Автореф. дисс. — Санкт-Петербург: СпбГУ29 с (2016).

Е. П. Буторина, Категорияофициальности в современномрусскомязыке. — Автореф. дисс. — РГГУ: Москва 38 с(2016).

М. Л. Лагутина, Глобальныйрегионкак элемент мировой политической системы XXI века (на примере Евразийского Союза). — Автореф. дисс. — Санкт-Петербург: СпбГУ, 45 с (2016).

МазуроваЛ., 2016. Иностранный как русский. — Литературная газета. — № 39 (6569), 5–11 октября 2016 г. — с. 18.

CHAPTER 17

Challenges in Fostering "People-to-People Bond": Studies on China by Southeast Asia and Studies on Southeast Asia by China

Ngeow Chow Bing

Institute of China Studies, University of Malaya,
Kuala Lumpur, Malaysia

17.1 Introduction

In 2013, the Chinese government put forward an ambitious plan of the Belt and Road (B&R) Initiative, which brings economic prosperity to China and nearly 60 countries along the road together. In order to achieve this goal, China proposed "Five connectivity": policy communication, facilities connectivity, unimpeded trade, financial integration, and people-to-people bond. As for people-to-people bond, President Xi Jinping pointed out that amity between people holds the key to sound relations between states. To make the B&R Initiative construction successful, we need to get the support from the people of the countries, strengthen the friendly exchanges among the people, enhance mutual understanding and traditional friendship, and lay a solid foundation of public opinion and social foundation to carry out regional cooperation. Vision and Actions on

Jointly Building Silk Road Economic Belt and 21st Century Maritime Silk Road, issued by the Chinese government in March 2015, provide a detailed description of people-to-people bond. The Chinese government and its leaders have expressed the importance of people-to-people bond, but generally speaking, academics, business, media, and other officials in China (and other countries) have not paid enough attention to study and understand the essence of people-to-people bond and figured out how to strengthen communication between the peoples. This chapter takes China's studies on Southeast Asia and Southeast Asia's studies on China as a case.

17.2 People-to-People Bond: Escort for "Other Four Connectivity"

In the *China's Economic Yearbook — The Belt and Road Initiative* volume, sponsored by Development Research Center of the State Council and issued in 2015, part of the content is about the research report of "the index of five connectivity among the B&R Initiative countries."[1] Each country will get "grades" based on "the index of five connectivity." As for people-to-people bond, the index system includes three aspects: tourism activities, science and technology exchanges, and non-governmental contacts, and further to refine and quantify in the aspect of the number of tourists, papers of scientific research cooperation, the number of Confucius Institute per million people, quantity of friendly cities, the degree of citizens' attention and so on.[2] This is the most quantitative research on the people-to-people bond currently. But the paper argues that the index system is still inadequate, although the number of tourists and the Confucius Institute is important, it cannot deeply reflect the understanding of a country to another country, nor to achieve the status of "people-to-people bond" The main reason is that the contribution of the intelligentsia/academia is still insufficient.

---

[1] China Economic Yearbook 2015 *The Belt and Road volume*, China's Economic Yearbook Press, 2015.

[2] The Southeast Asian countries have scored very high on the index of people-to-people bond. In the top 10 countries, there are 4 countries in Southeast Asia (Singapore, Thailand, Malaysia, Indonesia ranked first, second, fourth, and sixth, respectively).

Chinese scholar Li Ziguo pointed out the major strategic significance of "people-to-people bond" in a paper, including promoting strategic mutual trust, enhancing the openness of ideas, justifying bilateral economic and trade activities and expressing China's voice, etc. People-to-people bond cannot be effective in a short time, but it is of vital importance in the long term. At the same time, the paper also points out the current challenges in promoting people-to-people bond, including China's lack of international discourse rights, China's weakness in language and so on. Besides, the paper also puts forward some policy suggestions for people-to-people bond, such as the consensus-reaching and joint actions among industry, official and academia, talent training, and making good use of resources to tell China's story well.[3] Guo Xian-gang and Jiang Zhi-da, two scholars of the China Institute of International Studies, discuss the cognitive misunderstanding of "people-to-people bond" in another paper. They pointed out that "people-to-people bond" refers to the mutual communication, mutual understanding, and mutual recognition of the people, the countries, and the regions along the route, along with their goals, ideas, feelings, and civilizations. But there are a variety of cognitive misunderstandings, including that "people-to-people bond" means larger amount of money input, is purely a matter of government departments, and it is a deal with local governments and lack of enthusiasm with local people.[4] These views of Chinese scholars are very pertinent, pointing out the importance and shortcomings of the current work on "people-to-people bond." In particular, Li Ziguo's paper also mentioned that China must put itself in other countries' place. This is also emphasized in this chapter.

17.3 People-to-People Bond among the Academic/ Intellectual Circles in China and Southeast Asia

China and the Southeast Asian countries are neighbors, their relationship can be traced back to Zheng He's voyages to the western seas in the Ming

---

[3]Z.-G. Li, The blending point of people-to-people bond under the version of OBOR, *Journal of Xinjiang Normal University*, (3) (2016) 67–74.

[4]G. Guoxian and J. Zhida, People-to-people bond: Cognitive misunderstanding and developing methods, theories on ideas and understanding of OBOR, *Peace And Development*, (5) (2015) 1–11.

Dynasty. Some Southeast Asian countries (such as Vietnam) even have had relations with China for thousands of years. Today, however, the mutual understanding between the two sides (including the government, the enterprises, the academic circles, and the general public) is still insufficient, with much partiality and superficiality. One of the ideas in this chapter is that the research in academia and the reflection in intellectual circles serve as an important basis for mutual understanding. Here, the article is mainly inspired by Chinese scholar He Zhaotian's paper, "When China Began to Integrate with the World."[5] He proposed an important issue, that is, when China proposed the concepts of "win–win" and "harmonious world", he believes that those are the best things that can be shared with the rest of world. But in fact, its kindness could always be misunderstood.[6] Why? He further put forward a point of view, that is, "treat others in their way."[7]

And to effectively overcome the cross-cultural misunderstanding and the gap encountered by Chinese mainland people and make their kindness understood by their counterparts of the other side, it is necessary to really understand their history and culture.

The way to achieve all these is to "treat others in their way", other than treat others in a way that we think is good. This is in fact a kind of overlooking of the others.[8]

As He said, to really "treat others in their way", not only do we need to adjust our mind and faith, but practice it seriously. It is an idea that requires new knowledge and new understanding, which poses various challenges for our existing knowledge structure.[9]

He's paper has never mentioned the B&R Initiative or the people-to-people bond. This is the main problem of people-to-people bond: a lack

---

[5] H. Zhaotian, 2016. When China Began to Integrate with the World, Hong Kong: Inter-Asia School, pp. 15–49.

[6] H. Zhaotian, *When China Began to Integrate with the World* (Inter-Asia School, Hong Kong, 2016), p. 35.

[7] In fact, China has a wealth of traditional wisdom, including the similar ideas such as put oneself in others' position.

[8] H. Zhaotian, *When China Began to Integrate with the World* (Inter-Asia School, Hong Kong, 2016), pp. 35–36.

[9] H. Zhaotian, *When China Began to Integrate with the World* (Inter-Asia School, Hong Kong, 2016), pp. 36–37.

of new knowledge and understanding, which is also the thesis of the paper. The academic/intellectual community plays an indispensable role in building "people-to-people bond" between China and Southeast Asia. In the following paragraphs, we will discuss the China Studies on Southeast Asia and Southeast Asia Studies on China, especially on their shortcomings.

17.4 Studies on Southeast Asia by China

For a long time, there is no doubt that "Southeast Asia Studies", as a discipline, has been most developed in western countries (including Australia and Japan). Even scholars from Southeast Asia often go to the west to learn "Southeast Asia Studies." Of course, Southeast Asian countries also have outstanding scholars, but overall, except Singapore, "Southeast Asia Studies" by the western countries has become the mainstream. This, to a large extent, is because English is a global language. The scholars in Southeast Asian countries know about those scholars in the western countries who engage in "Southeast Asia Studies" as well as their achievements, because these academic achievements are generally written in English, and the common language of Southeast Asian academic circles is still English. Therefore, it is easy for scholars in Southeast Asia and in western countries to communicate with each other and make exchanges of personnel, network, and resources.

In contrast, in Southeast Asia, most Southeast Asian scholars have no idea what the opinions of the Chinese scholars on Southeast Asia are, except for some Chinese scholars who have access to and understand "Southeast Asia Studies" by the Chinese academia. Even if those Chinese scholars could basically communicate with Southeast Asian scholars in English, their academic achievements are still written in Chinese. There is no way for scholars from Southeast Asia and China to make in-depth exchange and obtain various academic resources, which often confines the Chinese scholars who are engaging in "Southeast Asia Studies" within a certain frame; as a Chinese phrase goes: "their feet are not on the ground".

The "Southeast Asia Studies" in China also has made great achievements and advantages. Since the achievements of the Chinese academia have not been paid much attention in Southeast Asia (apart from the Chinese scholars who can read Chinese in Southeast Asia), their achievements are often ignored by the mainstream of Southeast Asian Studies. In fact, Chinese scholars have done a good job in "Southeast Asia Studies", and have even done better than scholars from Southeast Asia and western countries in their dominant study fields (such as border-land history, Chinese, overseas Chinese studies, etc.)[10] But at the same time, it also caused some limitations. The shortcomings of "Southeast Asia Studies" in China include the following. First of all, there is still a lack of talents possessing high proficiency in Southeast Asia minority languages in Chinese academia. Most of the foreign language learners in China are still learning the language of the major western countries as well as Korean and Japanese. Although many Chinese universities (such as Beijing Foreign Studies University, etc.) also cultivate a lot of talent majoring in the Southeast Asia minority languages, a few of them move on to academia to become the main force in "Southeast Asia Studies". In this case, excellent researches can be made, but the limitations are obvious. For example, Chinese scholars who engage in studies on Malaysian Party Politics, as far as I know, mainly focus on Chinese political parties such as Malaysian Chinese Association (MCA) and Democratic Action Party (DAP), because they do not need to master the Malay language for researching these parties. Although these studies have done well, it is not sufficient to understand the political ecology of the political parties in Malaysia. Till now, no Chinese scholars have stud-ied in depth on the Malaysian Islamic Party, which has a far-reaching impact on Malaysian politics.

Second, Chinese scholars still lack field research at the grassroots level.

In the Southeast Asian countries, many academic institutions have many years of experience in receiving Western or Japanese scholars into the country as visiting scholars, some scholars even go into the rural areas, communities, and slums to get first-hand information, so that they can get the direct perception of the livelihood of the people, who live in

---

[10]Ten years ago, Institute of Southeast Asian Studies (ISEAS) in Singapore published *Southeast Asia Studies in China*, which is written in English. The book introduces Southeast Asia Studies in China in the most comprehensive way. S. Swee-Hock and W. John (eds.), *Southeast Asian Studies in China* (ISEAS, Singapore, 2007).

the bottom of the society in the Southeast, and can also have a more profound understanding of the country's politics, society, and economy. All of these resources cannot be acquired from the papers (or network).[11] In contrast, the Chinese scholars have little experience in this aspect. If any, it is usually confined to the scope of the study on the Chinese and overseas Chinese. Using again the expression that is mentioned above, the studies without grassroots experience have rarely set their feet on the ground.

Third, China's academic research on Southeast Asia is mainly concentrated on the southern universities, such as Xiamen University, Huaqiao University, Jinan University, Guangxi University, Yunnan University and so on. The Southeast Asian Studies converges in several universities that are geologically closer to these countries. There are inherent and intrinsic reasons, but it also conveys a concept, namely the Southeast Asian Studies is still around the edge of Chinese foreign policy. While the research on the United States, on Japan and on Europe often converge in the important political and economic centers such as Beijing and Shanghai, the Southeast Asian Studies are gathered in the frontier province, so that the young scholars in China would naturally think of Southeast Asian Studies as less important, but American and Japanese studies as a top priority. This also caused the shortage and fault of the talents in the field of the Southeast Asian Studies, which also leads to a gap in the overall quality of the Southeast Asian Studies between China and the countries like the United States and Japan.

Fourth, as these countries were a part of the ancient tributary system in history, the national records of the ancient Chinese dynasties in these countries are also important material in the recording of these countries' histories. Some of the Chinese scholars of the Southeast Asian history may sometimes have been subconsciously biased with the "China-centered" perspective, for which they may not have emphasized or even disregarded the historic view of the local academia or their historical

---

[11] For example, James C. Scott, the author of the Weapon of the Weak and Seeing Like a State is well known in the Chinese academica. He lived in the rural areas of Malaysia in his early age, and he refined the life experience of the local villagers into the academic concept of "the Weapons of the Weak".

materials. In the Chinese academia, the "China-centered" conception would not appear in the research on the United States, on Japan and on Europe, because these countries are the examples that China has wanted to learn from since modern times. But in Southeast Asian Studies, the concept of "China-centered" not only exists, but also affects the vision of the scholars, so that they lack the perspective of He Zhaotian's "correct cognition".

17.5 Studies on China by Southeast Asia

People-to-people bond is a two-way street. Therefore, China should treat Southeast Asia in their way and vice-versa. Southeast Asia should learn about Chinese history and reality and view China and the whole world from China's perspective. As there are many defects in China's studies on Southeast Asia, there are even more problems and defects in Southeast Asia's Studies on China. Scholars engaging in China Studies are not only small in quantity but uneven in quality. And for the non-Chinese scholars, language is a big challenge.

In my experience, the vast majority of think tanks and the academic community for strategy studies in Southeast Asia are very concerned about China. But the only way for them to understand China is by literature written in English. Therefore, they hold the one-sided understanding of China (often negative), although not "Anti-China", "suspicion" is the mainstream. At the same time, there is a lack of in-depth academic communication and exchange among scholars in Southeast Asian countries. In the 10 countries in Southeast Asia (excluding East Timor), the academic community for "China Studies" can be divided into four levels: (1) Singapore, (2) Vietnam, (3) Malaysia, Philippines, Thailand, Indonesia, and (4) Myanmar, Brunei, Cambodia and Laos.

17.6 Singapore

Among Southeast Asian countries, there is no doubt that Singapore alone does the best in "China Studies". There are many think tanks, research institutes, and universities, including East Asian Institute (EAI) of National University of Singapore (NUS), the Lee Kuan Yew School of Government, the Institute of International Studies of Nanyang Technological University, the Nanyang School of Public Administration, the School of Public Policy and International Affairs, ISEAS and so on. Besides, there are a variety of first-class talents, whose Academic works were published in English or Chinese so that their dialogues with the academic community in China and the rest of world are very active. Another difference between the China Studies by Singapore and by other Southeast Asian countries is the focus. In Singapore, few scholars engaging in "China Studies" do other researches that are irrelevant to China.[12] In other Southeast Asian countries, for a variety of reasons, scholars engaging in "China Studies" often do researches on local Chinese. Singapore's focus on "China Studies" makes it easier to do in-depth research. Singapore's "China Studies" is also characterized by its degree of internationalization, especially the early introduction of a lot of scholars from China and Hong Kong.[13] There are comparatively few local scholars in Singapore who engage in "China Studies." But in recent years the situation has gradually changed.

17.7 Vietnam

In Vietnam, the number of scholars involved in "China Studies" might be the most. As far as I know, there are over 80 scholars just in the Institute of "China Studies", Vietnamese Academy of Social Sciences. This does not include scholars who are dispersed in other research institutes in Vietnam. In June 2016, the Vietnamese National University in Hanoi set up a new course of "China Studies."[14] However, it is the most difficult to assess the quality of "China Studies" in Vietnam, because Vietnamese scholars rarely publish their academic works in other languages except Vietnamese. Therefore, it is difficult for scholars who do not understand Vietnamese to understand the degree of Vietnamese "China Studies." Most of the early Vietnamese scholars were sinologists, who have firm

---

[12]Except Wang Gung-wu, Liu Hong, etc.
[13]Such as Zheng Yongnian, from China and Huang Zhaohan from Hongkong.
[14]"China Studies Program Launched in Vietnam." Xinhua, June 10, 2016.

foundation in liberal arts but were not trained in modern social science.[15] Some western scholars who can understand Vietnamese have analyzed "China Studies" in Vietnam and found that the degree of "China Studies" in Vietnam is still low, beset by a couple of problems such as language barriers, lack of academic freedom, shortage of qualified personnel and so on.[16]

17.8 Malaysia, Philippines, Thailand, Indonesia

Basically, the "China Studies" in these four countries are at the same level. However, each country has its own difficulties in their "China Studies". Malaysia has only one research center dedicated to "China Studies", that is the Chinese Institute of Malaya University. It has been established for more than 10 years, and has developed well in the past two or three years, but on the whole, its academic performance is still far from satisfactory.[17] In fact, Malaysia has a good potential for the development of "China Studies": Most Malaysian Chinese have the best command of Chinese language in the Southeast Asian countries, and Malaysia–China relations have been relatively close. However, given the ethnic politics in Malaysia, most of the Chinese academic elites have devoted themselves to local Chinese research or literary studies, and there are few scholars involved in "China Studies", which has led to Malaysia being left behind by Singapore. However, in recent years, the Chinese Institute has attracted some Chinese scholars to join in and has improved the level of study. A serious problem at present is that it has failed to attract more Malay scholars to participate in the "China Studies", which is not a healthy phenomenon under the current ethnic situation in Malaysia. Fortunately,

---

[15]C.-Y. Shih, C.-C. Chou and H. T. Nguyen, Two intellectual paths that cross the borders: Nguyen Huy Quy, Phan Van Cac, and humanities in Vietnam's Chinese Studies, *East Asia: An International Quarterly*, **31**(2) (2014) 123–138.

[16]E. S. Ungar, China studies in the socialist Republic of Vietnam: Changes and implications, *Australian Journal of Chinese Affairs*, **16** (1986) 119–132; M. Sidel, The Re-emergence of China Studies in Vietnam, *China Quarterly*, **142** (1995) 521–540.

[17]As for the situation of Malaysia, please refer to my work, C. B. Ngeow, T. S. Ling and P. S. Fan, Pursuing Chinese studies amidst identity politics in Malaysia, *East Asia: An International Quarterly*, **31**(2) (2014) 103–122.

there are a number of young Malay scholars who can understand Chinese language and are dedicated to "China Studies" and they can become the new force of Malay academia in the future.

The Asian Center at the National University of the Philippines is home to a number of outstanding scholars in the Philippines, including the leading scholars for "China Studies", such as the renowned Professor Aileen S.P. Baviera. The Asian Center has taken in a number of dissidents in the era of Marcos government who have been exiled to China, which makes the institute quite distinctive. In addition to the National University of the Philippines, other universities with Chinese studies are De La Salle University and Ateneo de Manila University. De La Salle University has set up a position named "Chair in China Studies", which belonged to Renato Cruz De, a Philippine international relations scholar. Athenian University has a complete system of Chinese language teaching (including Confucius Institutes), Philippine and Chinese Studies, led by Ellen Palanca, another well-known Philippine scholar. In addition to these universities, the Philippines also has a national organization called Philippine Association for Chinese Studies, serving as a platform for all experts and scholars who have interest in "China Studies." Its current president Chito Sta. Romana is the Philippines "China hand".

The situation in Thailand is somewhat similar to that of Vietnam, where scholars involved in "China Studies" are not good at publishing their academic results in English or Chinese. In the past, Thailand had three highly respected and well-recognized scholars of "China Studies", Suebsang Promboon, Khien Theeravit, and Sarasin Viraphol.[18] After their retirement, the Thai academic research on China has weakened a lot. Thailand's two major academic centers, Chulalongkorn University and Hosei University, each has a number of Chinese research experts. Chulalongkorn University has an Asian Research Institute, under which a small-scale Chinese Research Center is established, the director is Vorasakdi Mahatdhanobol. Chulacheeb Chinwanno, Vice President of

---

[18] As for the academic life of the two latter scholars, please refer to P. Manomaivibool, Intellectual paths of Thailand's first generation China scholars: A research note on encountering and choices of Khien Theeravit and Sarasin Viraphol, *Asian Ethnicity*, **16**(1) (2015) 59–77.

Hosei University, is an expert on China's diplomacy. Actually, in Hosei University, there are many Chinese scholars, scattered in the Department of Political Science, Department of Economics, College of Interdisciplinary Studies and so on, but they rarely gather together to interact with one another. In addition to these two academic centers, Chia Tai Management Institute has a "China–ASEAN Institute", led by the Chinese scholar, Professor Zhimin Tang. Another private university, Rangsit University, also has a "Thai–China Institute".

Thai royal family (Princess Sirindhorn) has a good impression of China and Thai people have a passion for learning Chinese (There are nearly a thousand Thai students learning Chinese in the Institute of Sinology at Mae Fah Luang University, which is located in the northern part of Thailand). Therefore, Thailand has the largest number of and the most active Confucius Institute in Southeast Asia. However, language learning, after all, is only the foundation, which remains at a certain distance from "China Studies", the comprehensive discipline. One of Thailand's biggest problems with "China Studies", according to a young Thai scholar, is the lack of the concept of academic community, and academic exchange and communication are being ignored, which leads to a difficulty in the accumulation of the academics.

Indonesia is the most populous country in Southeast Asia, but its "China Studies" lags far behind the countries mentioned above, in addition to the era when Professor Ignatius Wibowo, the originator of Chinese studies, was alive. Professor Wibowo has worked on many academic works (including English and Bahasa Indonesia). His works cover many aspects of China's domestic and foreign affairs, including a thorough investigation into the rural areas of China. Professor Wibowo has also set up the first and the only academic unit for "China Studies" in Indonesia, Centre for Chinese Studies — Indonesia. Unfortunately, Professor Wibowo died at a young age. After his death, Center for Chinese Studies was inherited by scholar Natalia Soebagjo and the famous journalist Rene Pattiradjawane, but the Chinese study in Indonesia slowed down a lot. However, Indonesia's potential is perhaps the largest. From what I understand, over the past few years, a group of young scholars in Indonesia are studying for a doctor's degree in the first-class universities in China, Japan, Germany and other countries and writing doctoral papers on contemporary China. These scholars will be the new force in Indonesia.

The China Studies in all the four countries have some common problems: (1) in terms of research project, they usually pay attention to contemporary diplomatic relations or bilateral relations but there is a shortage in the study of China's domestic politics, economy, society, history, culture, philosophy, and other aspects; (2) scholars are not able to fully master the Chinese language; (3) the number of scholars in these four countries is far less than that of Singapore and Vietnam.

17.9 Brunei, Myanmar, Cambodia, and Laos

It can be concluded that there are few China Studies on Brunei, Myanmar, Cambodia, and Laos. Brunei, although a rich country, did not focus on developing the studies on contemporary China. The other three countries are among the 10 most underdeveloped countries in Southeast Asia, whose academic studies mainly focus on their own development and have no energy to cultivate experts for studies on foreign countries.

17.10 Policy Suggestions

From a revision of the studies on Southeast Asia by China as well as the studies on China by Southeast Asia, it can be argued that both should be improved, especially the latter (perhaps except Singapore). Here, we simply put forward some policy suggestions particularly for Chinese academia.

First, in terms of improving the studies on Southeast Asia, it is time to go out of the traditional preponderant field and expand to other areas. The study on overseas Chinese, cannot, of course, be abandoned, but the studies should not always be confined to this aspect. The understanding of the Southeast Asian countries must be comprehensive. At the same time, more scholars and graduate students should be encouraged to do research at the grassroots level in these countries by changing the previous research methods which rely on books, newspapers, and the Internet to obtain information.

Second, as for language training, language teaching should be integrated with studies on distinct regions or individual countries. At present, the foreign language teaching and regional research in China's universities seem to be two separate systems. Therefore, the academic centers of Southeast Asian Studies (Xiamen University, Jinan University, etc.) and centers of Southeast Asian language teaching (Beijing Foreign Studies University, Guangzhou University of Foreign Studies, etc.) are separate. In this case, most talents trained from language departments flow into the business community, media circle, or government, and rarely engage in academic research, leading to the long-term shortage of language talents in academic research.

Third, academic scholars from Southeast Asian countries should be directly introduced into China's academic units, encouraging Southeast Asian governments to set up Chair Professor for studies on individual countries in China's universities. The Malaysian government, for example, sets up a position of Chair Professor in Ohio University of the United States and employs Malaysian academic elites to teach and do research in the university. The Chair Professor does not teach language but engages in studies on individual countries.

Fourth, while studying the contemporary political, economic, social, and diplomatic issues in the Southeast Asian countries, we should not forget to study and understand the spiritual civilization and philosophical thinking of these countries. China is a country big on translation, where there are numerous world-famous masterpieces translated into Chinese. In my observation, China is only interested in translating western works (including Japanese works), so that the Chinese academics/intellectuals are very familiar with western philosophers, from Plato to Habermas. Meanwhile, the Chinese intelligentsia seems to be less interested in thinkers, philosophers, and intellectuals in non-western countries. Non-western thinkers, in fact, can often provide ideas for Chinese scholars. For example, Professor He Xutian, mentioned at the beginning of the paper, his paper was inspired by the Indian thinker, Nandy. At the same time, understanding the philosophers and thinkers of other countries is also an important channel to know the worldview and spiritual life of their people. Here, it is suggested that China publishes a series of "Translations of Southeast Asian Scholarly Works", with a focus on the translation or publication of influential works or anthologies of Southeast Asian thinkers or scholars.[19]

Finally, China is also playing an important role in improving the studies on Southeast Asia by China. The Chinese government is now providing a lot of scholarships for Southeast Asian graduate students to study in China, which is to be encouraged. However, in general, the doctoral dissertation written by them tends to be related to the development of their own country, or China's diplomacy or bilateral relations. These topics are important. However, Chinese professors should also encourage some students from Southeast Asia to study various issues of China, which is most needed at present for the studies on China by Southeast Asia.

17.11 Conclusion: The Importance of Mutual Studies in the Academic/Intellectual World for "People-to-People Bond"

In recent years, due to the South China Sea dispute, there have been many negative factors in China and Southeast Asian relations, especially for those who have sovereignty disputes with China. In my observation, China's intellectual thinkers or international relations academia, as well as their counterparts in the Southeast Asian countries, always lack a "simultaneous understanding of each other" in their comments of each other.[20] Actually, both sides should try to understand each other's demands, interests, and concerns in the South China Sea, and seek common ground under the circumstances of not violating their own stand of national interests, instead of taking care of their own stand point while ignoring the demands of the others'. In order to achieve "people-to-people bond" along the B&R Initiative, it is a necessary and fundamental work to improve the studies on Southeast Asia by China as well as the studies on China by Southeast Asia.

---

[19] For example, Malaysia's most famous sociologist Syed Hussein Alatas, his brother philosopher Syed Muhammad Naquib al-Attas and so on. Most of their writings are in English.

[20] N. Wei, *The Confusion of China's Rise and Developmentalism* (Asian Academy Press, Hong Kong, 2016), p. 62.

CHAPTER 18

Education Opportunities and Challenges under the Belt and Road Initiative

Chhun Hok

Royal University of Phnom Penh, Phnom Penh, Cambodia

18.1 Introduction

The Silk Road Economic Belt and the 21st Century Maritime Silk Road (MSR) are collectively known as the Belt and Road (B&R) Initiative. The B&R Initiative has been promoted inside and outside China by the Chinese Government to deepen and strengthen economic cooperation, trade deals, cultural, and educational activities. With reference to the B&R Initiative, we will discuss the opportunities and challenges.

18.2 Opportunities and Challenges

18.2.1 *Opportunities*

18.2.1.1 Regional Cooperation

The B&R Initiative's philosophy of connectivity and ideas of community of common interest, as well as community of common destiny, will bring regional cooperation to a new level and strengthen the role of multilateral cooperation mechanism.

18.2.1.2 Inclusive Globalization

The B&R Initiative brings another opportunity for Europe to change the world, rediscover its ties with China, take East–West integration to a new level, link Central Europe with Eastern Africa, and connect the Pacific and Indian oceans to the Mediterranean. Moreover, this new opportunity will create a more inclusive globalization and narrow down gaps between coastal and inland areas, and it also will give impetus to the development of China's western regions as well as Central Asia and Mongolia.

18.2.1.3 Global Development

The B&R Initiative is the major adjustment and transformation of the global and Chinese economies. Chinese economic development in the "new normal" adds new implications for the B&R Initiative. The progress of the initiative also provides development opportunities for the entire world.

18.2.2 Challenges

However, we can foresee some challenges, especially in some countries:

- First, we need to modernize ports, railroads, and ensure that the connectivity inside the country can also accommodate this initiative.
- Second, we have to ensure that the tourism sector will be equipped in other aspects, such as safety, cleanliness, protection including cultural and historical site protection.
- Third, we have to ensure that all the costs, especially transportation cost and electricity cost, benefit from the B&R Initiative.

18.3 Education Activities

Education plays an important role in a country's political, economic, and social development. In view of that, the educational institutions should make appropriate adjustments in their development strategies to meet the needs of social and economic development in different times. Depending on this reason, the advancement of globalization and the integration of knowledge and economy require all educational institutions and countries to modify their development strategies and orientations of education. So, they place the internationalization of education as top priority in their agendas.

Owing to the gap between the level of education and index for internationalization, all countries should develop their internationalization strategies so that they can actively merge into the B&R Initiative and promote their social, economic, cultural, and educational influence and competitiveness, in the following sections.

18.4 Government's Role and Leadership's Sense of Internationalization

The government should give enough attention to the guiding and leading role of education sectors. Furthermore, the implementation of the B&R Initiative requires the government and education institutions to be highly consistent in thought and action. So, the government should set up policies and provide as much financial support as possible to the educational institutions.

18.5 Internationalization Orientation on the Spirit of the B&R Initiative

Faced with the new requirements put forward by the implementation of the B&R Initiative, all educational institutions should grasp the essence of that strategy, and make appropriate adjustments in their development orientation on the thorough understanding of the economic and educational development tendency and demands of neighboring countries. Educational authorities should free their minds, enhance their sense of internationalization, make deeper reforms, and carry out educational internationalization though multichannels in multidomains.

18.6 International Cooperation in Education Field

The objectives of educational institutions should be as follows:

- find out problems in internationalization, analyze their causes and take effective measures related to the internationalization of the teaching staff, students' vision and exchange, and skills in economy, trade, tourism, and information technology and language;
- build a platform of international exchange and cooperation with educational institutions of neighboring countries involved in setting up offices in foreign countries, boosting transnational education, and sharing education resources;
- send scholars and students to study abroad, and establish relationship with foreign educational institutions;
- promote the educational internationalization concerning the enrollment scale of international students, the use of regional advantages of educational resources, and students with high-quality education resources and services;
- strengthen communication with other countries to create a kind of international atmosphere on campus and enhance the sense of internationalization of their teachers and students.

18.7 Royal University of Phnom Penh

Ever since China raised the concept of the B&R Initiative, this initiative has received warm welcome and attention from the international community including Cambodia.

The B&R Initiative will give power to the respective countries in terms of economic, educational, and social development and sustainability. The B&R Initiative also strongly holds the principals of negotiation, cooperation, and mutual assistance. Since a long time ago, Cambodia and

China have had mutual understanding, trust and support for each other. Moreover, the B&R Initiative has provided a new opportunity for Cambodia and China to open a new chapter of cooperation and the implementation of the B&R Initiative in Cambodia requires time and shall align with the people's will.

As for the education activities, the B&R Initiative provides new opportunities as in the following sections.

18.8 Opportunities for Education Sectors

Based on the requirements of economy and social development, the education sectors should carry out the following:

- The education sector are responsible for training personnel, promoting cultural exchange, deepening international exchange, and cooperation with education sectors in other countries.
- The education sectors have to expand the exchange and cooperation in the fields of agriculture, medical science, forestry, education, economy, and trade, and bring up more students with international awareness to cater to regional economy and social development.

18.9 Influence of Internationalization of Education Sectors

We do our best to promote bilateral and multilateral education sectors' alliance; set up exchange education platforms and research institutes; build exchange platforms for researching programs on issues of politics, economy, culture, environment, and social science; and map out an overall planning of Chinese language setup in Cambodia.

18.10 Level of Education Sector Management and Development Opportunities

We intensify the management of cooperative education and complete quality guarantee system, the teaching quality can be enhanced, and deepen bilateral and multilateral cooperation in educational sectors, enhance educational connections, and promote culture exchange with China.

18.11 New Win–Win Models/Strategies in Education Field

To meet the opportunities and challenges mentioned above, we do our best to promote bilateral and multilateral cooperation:

Under the support from the Chinese Government, the Royal Government of Cambodia set up the Confucius Institute in 2009. Moreover, under the bilateral cooperation between Dali University and Royal University of Phnom Penh (RUPP), the Chinese Center was set up in 2007 and the Chinese Department in 2010.

RUPP played a key role in sharing and increasing the awareness of history, languages, culture, education, and common values. As a member of ASEAN Universities Network, RUPP has been actively involved with and participated in many meaningful events regionally and globally in order to enhance mutually beneficial educational partnership.

More significantly, RUPP has a strong international focus. It has signed Memoranda of Understanding (MoU) on academic cooperation, staff, and student exchanges, cultural relations and curriculum development assistance with many international universities. Up to date, RUPP holds active MoUs with universities and research centers in many countries, especially in China, such as The Hong Kong Polytechnic University, Dali University, Honghe University, Yuxi University, Beijing Foreign Studies University, Guangdong University of Foreign Studies, Guangxi Normal University, Guangxi University of Nationalities, Kunming University, Minnan Normal University, South University of Science and Technology, Yunnan Nationalities University, Yunnan Normal University, Tianjin Sino-German University of Applied Science, Nanjing Institute of Railway Technology, Beijing Jiaotong University, Guiyang Vocational and Technical Institute, etc.

Responding to the establishment of the B&R Initiative, RUPP set up a Cambodia Maritime Silk Road Research Center on 13 June 2016 to meet the objectives of the initiative.

18.12 Vision of Center

The vision of the Center is to interpret, inform, and influence developments and policy making for the benefits and interests of Cambodia in all areas of the 21st Century MSR.

18.13 Goal

The overall goal is to establish a center that will support connectivity and facilitate a better understanding of the 21st Century MSR. The Center envisions itself as a sustainable resource center serving Cambodian policymakers, scholars, students, professionals, and the general public on issues related to connectivity between China and Southeast Asia.

18.14 Project Objectives

- To promote intensive learning about the 21st Century MSR by Cambodian graduates and undergraduates, as well as research among Cambodian scholars on the topic of the Maritime Silk Road;
- To provide training courses for "connectivity professionals" on diplomatic, business, economic, and cultural approaches of the Maritime Silk Road;
- To advance the exchange of view on President Xi's "neighborhood diplomacy" through win–win cooperation and connectivity among Chinese scholars/officials, Cambodian government officers and Cambodian and regional researchers.

18.15 Main Functions of Center

The Center has the following main functions:

- **Teaching:** The Center focuses on teaching and research with the emphasis on connectivity and the B&R Initiative, particularly the 21st Century MSR, mainly to both undergraduate and graduate students of RUPP, and also to students of other universities in Cambodia via short intensive and certificate courses.
- **Researches:** The Center has broad programs within its research component:
  ○ Political and Strategic Program
  ○ Economic and Financial Program
  ○ Social, Cultural, and Environmental Program

- **Training and Workshop:**
  - To keep Cambodia in the attention of China and regional foreign policymakers;
  - To make available the fruits of research on connectivity and the 21 Century MSR;
  - To bring attention to questions which are important, but neglected in public debate;
  - To give important officials in the country an opportunity to present their views to a wider audience;
  - To provide China and Cambodia forums to conduct their public, economic, and development diplomacies.

18.16 Publications and Dissemination

The Center creates various platforms for publication and dissemination of its research to large and varied audiences consisting of policymakers, academia, and educated public.

In conclusion, the B&R Initiative provides a broader space for us to develop the educational institutions; meanwhile, it brings about new opportunities and challenges for development. Under this circumstance, all educational institutions should make their internationalization strategy by analyzing the advantages and disadvantages, the opportunities and challenges brought about by political, social, economic, and technological situations of internationalization, clarifying corresponding development strategy and forging appropriate function modes for government and educational institutions.

Further Reading

J. Su-IL, *The Silk Road's Encyclopedia* (Korean Institute of Civilizational Exchanges, 2016).

W. Yiwei, *The Belt and Road Initiative-What will China Offer the World in its Rise* (New World Press, 2015).

International Cooperation and Exchange Office, *Chinese International Education in the Context of Globalization* (Dali University, 2016).

Department of International Study, *The Belt and Road Initiative and Its Implications for Cambodia* (Royal University of Phnom Penh, 2016).

Study Office, *Hand Book 2012–2016* (Royal University of Phnom Penh), 2016.

Part 4

Views on the Belt and Road Initiative from Chinese Scholars

CHAPTER 19

The Belt and Road Initiative: The Chinese Wisdom

Wang Yiwei

School of International Relations, Renmin University of China, Beijing, China

Introduction

"Magnificent time needs magnificent pattern, magnificent pattern needs magnificent wisdom."[1] It was for managing the grand stage of the Eurasia, and the magnificent pattern of the world that President Xi Jinping proposed the Belt and Road (B&R) Initiative. Jointly constructing the B&R Initiative is in line with the fundamental interests of the international community. It is an active exploration for the new model of international cooperation and global governance.

19.1 What is B&R?

The "B&R" is the abbreviation for the "Silk Road Economic Belt" and the 21st Century "Maritime Silk Road." In September 2013, during his visit to Kazakhstan, Chinese President Xi Jinping released the

---

[1] X. Jinping, Speech at Opening Ceremony of the APEC CEO Summit, November 9 2014.

important speech titled "Carry forward the Friendship between the Peoples and Create a Better Future Together" at the Nazarbayev University. In his speech, President Xi pointed out, "In order for the Eurasian countries to have closer economic ties, deeper cooperation, and broader space for development, we can build the 'Silk Road Economic Belt' together with innovative model of cooperation to gradually form a grand regional cooperation, for which we can start from points to areas, from lines to regions."

19.2 The Chinese Principle: Jointly Build through Consultation to Meet the Interests of all

The B&R Initiative, relying on the existing bilateral and multilateral mechanism between China and the countries along it, by means of the existing and effective regional cooperative platform, actively develops economic cooperation partnership with the countries along it to cross over the zero-sum game by achieving win–win situation.

The B&R Initiative upholds the principle of openness and inclusiveness and advocates the idea of jointly building through. Consultation to meet the interests of all, which are as follows: China and the countries along the B&R seek for the docking of projects, funds, technology, and standards, work together to build a community of common interest in mutual political trust, economic integration, and cultural inclusiveness.

China advocates "joint discussion" to respect the rights of speech of countries along the B&R during their participation in distinct projects and properly handle the interests among the countries in the course of constructing the B&R Initiative. At the same time, China advocates "joint construction".

19.3 The Chinese Philosophy: The Unity of Knowledge and Practice

The Chinese ancient philosophers believed that the extension of intuitive knowledge and the unity of knowledge and practice are the core of Chinese philosophy. The construction of the B&R Initiative vividly reflects this philosophy of China.

19.4 The Chinese Ethics: Mutual Prosperity and Support

The Chinese ethics revealed in the above dialogue are reflected by the B&R Initiative, and the Asian Infrastructure Investment Bank, and by that China has become the world's second largest economy after over 30 years of reform and opening-up.

As the General Secretary Xi Jinping put it at the Working Conference for Promoting the Construction of the B&R Initiative, "insist on jointly building through consultation to meet the interests of all: follow equality; pursue mutual benefit; firmly grasp the key direction; focus on the key areas, the key countries, the key projects, and seize the development of the greatest common divisor to not only benefit the Chinese people, but also the people in the countries along the B&R. Various countries and international organizations are welcome to ride with us on the express bandwagon of China development and to participate in the cooperation."[2] It was based on this understanding that I had it printed on the back cover of my work, One Belt One Road: Opportunity and Challenge, "the World Raised China, China is Giving Back to the World."[3]

19.5 The Chinese Strategy: Achieving the Medium by Aiming the Highest

The B&R Initiative sets its foothold to comprehensively deepen the reform and all-round opening (listed in the three grand development strategies with the Yangtze River Economic Belt and the Beijing–Tianjin–Hebei Integration) inside the China; together with the Free Trade Agreement of the Asia Pacific (FTAAP), it constitutes the grand strategy with "one body and two wings" to accomplish the Chinese dream.

---

[2] Xinhua News Agency, Beijing, August 17, 2016
[3] W. Yiwei, *One Belt One Road: Opportunity and Challenge* (People's Publishing House, 2015).

19.6 The Chinese Tactics: Unite the East and the West, Link the Land and the Sea

Some people recon the B&R Initiative as China's countermeasure of the "west strategy" against the pivot to Asia by the US. The B&R Initiative bases its wisdom from the game go, focuses on the big picture, ignores the gain or loss in a spot while seeking to win over the whole board.

Some people from the west forecast that poverty and political instability in those countries of Southeast Asia and Central Asia that are included in the B&R Initiative will lead it to failure. The B&R Initiative's concept of President Xi Jinping is based on the notion that "the nation will win for sure as long as it is interconnected with its peripheral countries", namely, the Go playing strategy of winning the game through occupying the areas at the other three sides on the board. Another feature of Go is of protracted warfare. The Chinese generally believe that time is on their side.[4]

19.7 The Chinese Experience: The Chinese Paradigm of Revolution — Construction — Reformation and Opening

From the perspective of either the top-level design or the concrete practice, the various stages of the Chinese revolution, construction, and reform produced a series of methods, experiences, and models of Chinese characteristics.

The forming of a "comprehensive open system" by the B&R Initiative refers to the promotion of a new round of opening-up. It will achieve "upgrade" in the following four aspects:

First is the aspect of opening-up. The B&R Initiative does not set limit to the "ID" for the participating parties. It is open to countries along it and also to countries and entities that participate in it in other forms.

Second is the aspect of opening-up. The B&R Initiative requires formulating an opening policy toward broader domestic and international market.

---

[4]L. Shangzhe. The Go Like Xi Jinping diplomacy, *Central Daily*, Korea, 3 June, 2015.

The third aspect refers to the forms of interaction. The opening-up is to better realize bilateral or multilateral economic interactions.

The fourth aspect refers to the open state of mind. By construction of the B&R Initiative, China is advocating for the opening up of inclusiveness, carrying forward pragmatic cooperation of inclusiveness, and leading the new trend of international cooperation.

19.8 The Chinese Path: Coordination of Overall Planning

In accordance with the requirements of General Secretary Xi Jinping, the construction of the B&R Initiative must plan and coordinate, adhere to coordination between land and sea, between domestic and overseas, between government and enterprise; encourage domestic enterprises to invest and operate in countries along the B&R; strengthen the coordinated development of the B&R construction and the Beijing–Tianjin–Hebei region, and docking with the national strategies, such as the Yangtze River Economic Belt.

19.9 The Chinese Formula: Connectivity

In October 2014, at the Dialogue on Strengthening Connectivity Partnership between Host Partners, President Xi Jinping put forward in his speech that if the B&R Initiative is seen as the two wings for Asia's take-off, connectivity should be seen as the bloodline of the two wings.

The B&R Initiative stresses on "five connectivity" — policy communication, facilities connectivity, unimpeded trade, financial integration, and the people-to-people bond — to create a new pattern of systematic networking and humane connectivity. It applies the same philosophy as the traditional Chinese medication which stresses on opening up the conception vessel and the governor vessel.[5]

The first connectivity aspect is policy communication. For this purpose, we should strengthen intergovernmental cooperation, actively build

---

[5] W. Yiwei, *The World Is Connected: The Logic of One Belt One Road* (Commercial Press, 2016).

communication mechanism for multilevel intergovernmental macro-policies, deepen interest integration, improve mutual political trust, and achieve new consensus for cooperation.

The second aspect is facilities connectivity. It mainly includes four categories. The first is transportation infrastructure — prioritize deficient road segments, bottleneck road segments, and provide perfect road safety facilities and traffic management facilities to improve the access and passage level of the road. The second is port infrastructure, namely, smooth land and water transport channels, improve the cooperative construction of the ports and increase the sea routes and frequency to strengthen information cooperation in maritime logistics. The third is energy infrastructure. The fourth is cross-border communication network, such as optical cable.

Third is the unimpeded trade. The relevant parties should discuss and make arrangements for the facilitation of trade and investment, eliminate trade barriers, reduce costs for trade and investment, and improve the speed and quality of the regional economic circulation to realize mutual benefit and win–win results. The cooperation in investment and trade is the key content in the construction of the B&R Initiative.

The fourth aspect is financial integration. The Vision and Action of Promoting the Joint Construction of the Silk Road Economic Belt and the 21st Century Maritime Silk Road illustrates that financial integration is an important pillar for the construction of the B&R Initiative.

The fifth connectivity aspect refers to strengthening the people-to-people bond; promote the formation and diffusion of the concept of inclusiveness and openness through the cultural exchange.

In general, the Silk Road spirit of "peaceful cooperation, open and inclusive, learning from each other, mutual benefit and win–win" is the crystallization of the wisdom of the Chinese history.

19.10 The B&R Wisdom

An article published in the Guide, Russia, put forward that the idea of the B&R Initiative reveals China's thinking on new ideas of global governance. "To China, instead of being a road, the B&R Initiative is more like the most important philosophical category, Tao."

19.11 Sharable — Win–Win — Philosophy

The B&R Initiative is both the gripper for the transformation of the Chinese economic development model and the accountability of China as a big nation state.

President Xi Jinping has given a classic description of win–win philosophy, "it is peace instead of war, cooperation instead of confrontation, win–win instead of zero-sum, that is the eternal theme of a peaceful, progressive, and developing world." Professor Hu Angang concluded that, "the most distinct difference from colonialism, imperialism, and hegemony is that the former is injustice, while the latter integrative; the former is discriminatory, while the latter is equal; the former is exclusive, while the latter is inclusive."[6]

The Chinese proposition of China and Arab is to jointly construct the B&R Initiative, build a "1 + 2 + 3" cooperation pattern with energy cooperation as its principal axis, with the infrastructure construction and the facilitation of trade and investment as the two wings, with the three new high-tech fields of nuclear energy, aerospace satellite, and new energy as breakthrough, and strengthen the cooperation of production capacity that has received positive response from the Arab states.

With the adjustment of the world economy structure and the development of the global economy, China is transforming from being the factory of the world that produces general consumer goods to the production base that provides the world with advanced equipment.

The B&R Initiative is also carrying forward this tradition by adhering to the idea of "two inclusiveness", "two division", and "one grasp".

The "two inclusiveness" refers first to the compatibility with the existing local cooperation framework, avoiding the setting up of a separate kitchen. Second, to be inclusive to the powers outside of the region, instead of excluding those powers, such as Russia, Europe, Japan, etc.

The "two division" refers to a reasonable division of labor and division of responsibility, instead of being in charge of everything by one party.

---

[6]H. Angang, The One Belt One Road economic geographic revolution and the era of win-winism, *Guangming Daily*, July 16, 2015.

The "one grasp" refers to catching hold of the terminal of the Silk Road, Europe; promote China–EU maritime cooperation, devote common efforts to the "five connectivity"; manage the risk control of the B&R Initiative.

19.12 Sustainable Development: Intergenerational Equilibrium

Humankind — from east to west, from north to south — is facing the challenges in achieving sustainable development.

After the collision with the west for over a hundred years, now, for the first time, China is standing at the same starting line in many aspects, facing a lot of same or similar problems, such as the problem for sustainable development, problem for ecological environment, etc.

The B&R Initiative is to start with the major common concerns of humankind and focus on the general significance of sustainable development. The trinity of sustainable development, sustainable livelihood, and sustainable thinking is the connotation of the era for sustainable development.

Sustainable development is to be inclusive to achieve equality between the early starters and the latecomers, between the big powers and the small nations, and between generations, to change the *status quo* of the west being not inclusive toward others to optimize the balance between development and consumption, and between will and power.

By implementing sustainable development, China provides the world with the "Chinese model" of sustainable development. This is China's strongest international voice today. This is the mission of the B&R Initiative in terms of theory and practice.

According to the calculation, during 2010–2020, the infrastructure investment demand of the Asian developing countries is as much as US$ 8 trillion, with an average annual investment demand for over US$ 700 billion, and the existing annual investment in the field of infrastructure in Asia by the multilateral development banks is only around US$ 10–20 billion. In this case, by establishing the AIIB to mobilize more funds to support the infrastructure construction and connectivity within the region, it will inject long-term momentum for Asian economic growth and will also contribute to the benevolent economic interaction between China and the neighboring countries.

The AIIB is not only stimulating the reform of the international financial system, but also starting a new path of global governance for the 21st Century: lean, clean, green. Just as President Xi Jinping pointed out, "the establishment and operation of the AIIB have important significance to the reform and perfection of the global economic governance system. It conforms to the adjustment and transformation trend of world economic structure, and is helpful to promoting global economic governance system toward a more just, fair, and effective direction."

19.13 Internalization: Taking Root

The B&R Initiative is the sinification, modernization, and popularization of the ancient Silk Road. Taking root is the requirement of popularization. Being fruitful is the necessary goal for the shared development.

How to construct the B&R Initiative? President Xi Jinping spoke of the "five connectivity". It is emphasized again that the B&R Initiative is not for enterprises to "go out", but "go into". Namely, they should touch the ground and combine with the local development projects.

Soejima Taneomi, a Japanese sinologist, said, "as for all the inveteracy of China, there are always feasible methods, but there are no people to implementing by the methods; there are wonderful words, but there are no practices to putting them into effects." In other words, the methods that are applied to practice without talented people are only empty talks. This is a warning to us.

Lee Kuan Yew put it this way: China is still selecting talents from the 1.3 billion population, while the US is choosing talents from the 7 billion population. Now in the course of constructing the B&R Initiative, we should pick up talents from the 4.4 billion population, integrating wisdom of the 65 countries to converge the world wisdom through openness, inclusiveness, and win–win cooperation.

That Chinese come out of the modern history and bid farewell to the west will definitely encourage the people of the countries along the B&R to the same direction, so as to make it really happen where every country enjoys what it has instead of envying what the west has, and that they achieve the common rejuvenation of various civilizations and the common development of different countries.

CHAPTER 20

The Dual-Track Drive of Trading and Humanity — Reflection on the Construction of the Belt and Road

Yang Zhengwei

*The Center for Development Strategy and Public Policy,
Chinese Academy of Governance (CAG), China*

20.1 Introduction

Reviewing the ancient Silk Road and looking at the Silk Road today, the ancient Silk Road was never exclusive and enclosed, but inclusive and open; the construction of the Silk Road today should also be like this. At present, various projects of the Silk Road intersect a lot with numerous points of common interest. We can seek for the maximized intersection of its various versions through various platforms and exchange mechanisms. It is the strategy of our nation in implementing the new round of opening up to promote the construction of the contemporary Silk Road. By summing up the historical experience and synthesizing the current international environment, the construction of the Silk Road needs to take the path of pragmatic cooperation, follow the guidance of the government and the decisions of the market, allow the enterprises to be the principal part, let economic and trading cooperation to be the forerunner, and connect the modern Silk Road in the grand area.

20.2 The Inclusiveness of the Silk Road

The ancient Silk Road of China explicitly reveals that the Silk Road has the following functions.

First, it is a road of trade. The Silk Road was a commercial trade corridor. The outflows from China by the trade caravans were mainly silk, golden, and silver wares; the inflows into China were mainly jewelry, spices, medicinal materials, and farming products like grape, flax, etc. The exchange was mainly among high-end luxury products. Silk became as expensive as gold upon arriving in Rome after switching trade for couple of times. The commercial interest made it possible for the motivation of the long distance transportation and its sustainability. The commerce and sea trade were well developed in Song Dynasty, so that its economy and technology reached the peak of the feudalist era. Though the road was the most unimpeded during the Mongolian Empire, the civil trade was underdeveloped, it did not contribute to the national power and did not maintain long enough. The seven voyages to the western seas in the early Ming Dynasty were only of political purpose for advocating the national pride without the active civil trade. It caused the decline of national power and its glory was transitory. The tributary trade system with the vassal states declined as it became a heavy burden on the government and people as it breached the normal rules of economics. Therefore, without economic and trade foundation, lacking the free flow of commodity, the Silk Road cannot be sustained through pure political and cultural exchange.

Second, it is a road of opening-up. The prosperous Silk Road happened in the most open periods of China, Han Dynasty, Tang Dynasty, Song Dynasty, and Yuan Dynasty. China at those times was open and confident. The two Silk Roads in Tang Dynasty were both well developed. It was so open that foreigners were allowed to take the imperial examination to become officials. Most of its major generals were of minority ethnicities. The rise and fall of the Silk Road is the thermometer for the strengths and weaknesses of the dynasties of the Central China Plain. The prosperous times of the land and sea Silk Roads were always the most prosperous times of China. In 1492, carrying the letter of credence to the Chinese Emperor and the Indian King, Columbus hoped that his voyage could eventually reach China.

Third, it is the envoy that delivers peace. The Silk Road of China was formed and extended in the ancient times of the prosperous and powerful China; China did not use it for invasion and expansion. It revealed China's goodwill of its tributary system and benevolent governance; it verified China's historical tradition of peaceful development. During the times when the land Silk Road was unimpeded, there was basically no chaos of war in regions along it. But in the turning of East Han Dynasty and Sui Dynasty, from the Mid-Tang Dynasty to the beginning of Yuan Dynasty, there were long terms of war and continued ethnical conflicts in the northwest; the Silk Road was blocked from time to time. During over 1,000 years since the prosperity of the Maritime Silk Road in Tang Dynasty and Song Dynasty, it had been a road of peace for China and various countries.

Fourth, it is a road of civilization. The Silk Road traversed the time and space for 2,000 years, going across various countries in Asia, Europe, and Africa.

Therefore, the Silk Road brought not only trade and prosperity, but also the "byproducts" such as cultural exchange, technology communication, and religious spreading.

20.3 Antecedence of Economy and Trade

In the recent over 30 years, China's opening up was mainly concentrated in the coastal areas. Around 90% of import and export, 85% of foreign capital, and 75% of overseas investment are concentrated in the east; the opening up of the land route is clearly lagging behind. Extending the opening westward and constructing the Silk Road will help optimize the layout of China's space for opening-up, make the western region become the "vanguard" from the "backup team", and promote all-round pattern of opening with the cooperation between the eastern and western regions, and the paralleled advancement at land and sea. Meanwhile, in the era of maritime rights, Central Asia and the western region of China are marginalized to be the "sagging zone" between the two economic zones of Asia–Pacific and Europe. This leads to the imbalanced international development and breeds the three forces, such as terrorism, which threaten the peace of human society.

In recent years, the railway and highway technology have improved rapidly, especially the high-speed rail road has reached a speed of 350 km/h, which greatly decreases the cost for land transportation, and provides technological support for raising the priority of road rights.

There is an urgent need to ensure the efficient and sustainable road transportation. Road building is motivated by large volume of trade. China's average speed of cargo railway is 80 km with the speed designed to be 120–160 km, but in trains, such as Chongqing–Xinjiang–Europe railway, the average speed is less than 30 km. The reason lies in the inconvenience of custom clearing. It further lies in lack of cargo, which seriously affects the efficiency and cost of the transportation management.

20.4 The Leadership of the "New Silk Road"

Since the 1980s, the related international institutions and countries have proposed projects for exploring the Silk Road and have achieved certain progress. The UN launched quite a few silk road projects in 1988. The Asian Infrastructure Investment Bank (AIIB) initiative established the mechanism of regional economic cooperation in Mid Asia; the International Union of Railways (IUR) proposed "Silk Road Rejuvenation Project." The US proposed the "New Silk Road Project" in 2011; Russia proposed the "Railway Silk Road Project" in 2013.

The prospect of the contemporary Silk Road has attracted the attention from all over the world. There are different versions of new Silk Road or modern Silk Road projects.

First is the "New Silk Road Project" of the US. The US proposed the "Silk Road Strategy" in 1999 and 2006. It proposed the "New Silk Road Project" in 2011, aiming at taking Afghanistan as the hub, having South Asia, Central Asia, and West Asia connected to realize "energy southward, commodity northward", to realize the transformation "from aid to trade", to improve the economic viability and sustain its influence in Central Asia. Its advantage lies in its dominance power, western support, interest equilibrium, and relatively high enthusiasm from various parties. Its disadvantage lies in that it goes through the unsecured regions, hardship in connectivity westward by having Iran excluded, and the sustainability of the project is also questioned.

Second are the new Silk Road and the Eurasian Union of Russia. Russia called the first and second Eurasian continental bridge as the "New Silk Road", and claimed that it would play a decisive role in the construction of the Silk Road. In fact, what Russia promoted was the Eurasian Union on the basis of Russia–Belarus–Kazakhstan customs union. The advantage of the Eurasian Union lies in the traditional ties, strong mechanism, but the disadvantages are that the economic complementarity is not strong, there is lack of economic driving force, plus the suspicion of reviving the empire, which lead to the concerns raised by the world, in particular Central Asia.

The third is the Silk Road project such as the North–South Corridor. Russia, India, and Iran launched the "North–South Corridor" in September 2000. Then as China and all the Central Asian countries joined in, it transformed into a 14-nation initiative. This corridor overlaps a lot with the US "New Silk Road Project." In August 2012, Afghanistan, India, and Iran discussed about the new "South Silk Road" connecting Iran, Central Asia, and South Asia. In addition, there are also other ones with considerable influence, such as the "Silk Road Diplomacy" by Japan, the "Central Asia New Partnership Relations" by the EU, and the "Connecting Central Asia" new strategy of India.

The fourth version includes the Silk Road project of the international organizations. The UN was the earliest international organization that proposed reviving the "Silk Road". In 1988, the "Comprehensive Research on Silk Road — the Road of Dialogue" project was launched. From 1992 to 2005, the UN implemented quite a few infrastructure projects intending to rebuild the "silk road". At the Euro-Asia Economic Forum 2008, launched by the UNDP and responded by 19 countries, The International Road Federation (IRF) proposed in 1998 the "Reviving the Silk Road" project. The Asian Development Bank earlier proposed the Central Asia regional economic cooperation project, which is analogous to the new Silk Road.

Comparing the various projects, their contents are intersected. The above-mentioned projects and the Silk Road zone of China overlap a lot in contents, especially in economic and trade cooperation and road construction; they concentrate the most in Mid-Asia scalewise, and spread around. All the different versions of "Silk Road" recognize Central Asia as the economic and political hub that connects Europe and Asia with logistics and resources and hope that they can build "seamless connectivity" with this hub, so that they can explore their trade route and economic circle more effectively; and expand their externality of economy, energy, and security.

CHAPTER 21

Research on Differential Strategies of the Belt and Road Initiative Implemented by Each FTZ

Xu Peiyuan

Maritime Silk Road Institute, Huaqiao University,
Quanzhou, China

21.1 Introduction

The construction of the Free Trade Zones (FTZs)[1] and the strategy of the Belt and Road (B&R) Initiative are part of version 2.0 of China's opening up to simultaneously promoting the grand strategy of the integration both at home and abroad. The opening up of China at the current stage consists of three major objects: perfection of the open economy system; construction of the new system of the open economy; nurture and lead the new competitive advantage of the international economic cooperation.

---

[1]The FTZ in this chapter refers to its definition in a narrow sense, namely, a special economic zone focusing on trade inside the territory while outside the customs, within the sovereignty of a nation state.

21.2 The B&R Initiative and Free Trade Zone

21.2.1 *The B&R Initiative*

During his visit to Central Asia in September 2013, President Xi Jinping proposed to jointly construct the Silk Road Economic Belt. During his visit to Southeast Asia in October the same year, President Xi Jinping expressed the wish to jointly construct the Maritime Silk Road (MSR) of the 21st century by enhancing maritime cooperation with the ASEAN countries. The Silk Road Economic Belt and the 21st century MSR are referred to in abbreviation as the B&R Initiative, which covers East Asia, Central Asia, Southeast Asia, South Asia, West Asia, Africa, and parts of Europe. The core contents in the construction of the B&R Initiative include policy communication, facility interconnection, unimpeded trade flow, accommodation of funds, and people-to-people bond. The objective of the B&R Initiative is to concatenate the key ports, center cities, and industrial parks through infrastructures to promote the liberalization of investment and trade and eventually build a network of global FTR by starting from the peripheral regions and radiating gradually toward the regions along the B&R.

21.2.2 *Free Trade Zone*

It was in September, 2013, that the Shanghai FTR was established officially. The construction of FTR is another important strategy of China facing the new rules and new pattern of international investment and trade.

Currently, as the WTO multilateral trading system has halted with hesitation, the US is promoting negotiation for the Trans-Pacific Partnership Agreement (TPP), The Transatlantic Trade and Investment Partnership (TTIP), and Trade in Services Agreement (TISA), re-making the rules for international trade and investment to shape the "high standard sample for free trade rules of the 21st century"; China faces a severe test in participation in global trade and investment.

The core content in the construction of the FTZ is liberalization of investment, facilitation of trade, internationalization of financing, and legalization of administration.

21.3 The Free Trade Zone of the B&R Initiative

The FTZ is the domestic strategic fulcrum of the B&R Initiative. It hosts the task of implementing the B&R Initiative, acting as the points, the pieces, and the units. The FTZ and the B&R are the pieces and complement each other.

21.3.1 *The Conjunction of the FTZ and the B&R Initiative*

The four big FTZs are the core areas of the B&R Initiative. Shanghai, Guangdong, Tianjin, and Fujian are the economic hubs of China. The layout of the four big FTZs has comparatively strong function for the economic radiation and connectivity of the core domestic areas and the related countries of the B&R Initiative. The "five connectivity" (policy communication, facility connectivity, unimpeded trade flow, integrated financing, and people-to-people bond) that was proposed by General Secretary Xi Jinping on account of the B&R Initiative is connected spiritually to the four principles of the FTZ (liberalization of investment, facilitation of trade, internationalization of financing, legalization of administration).

The B&R Initiative and the FTZ construction are the body and wings of China's opening; they are the important contents for building the new pattern of China's comprehensive opening.

21.4 The Docking of the B&R Initiative and the FTZ

The construction of the FTZ should dock with the B&R Initiative. (1) The innovation for the system mechanism of the FTZ is to conform to the regulations and directions of the B&R trade and economic cooperation. (2) By making use of their competitive advantage, each FTZ should implement the B&R Initiative in differentiation. (3) With facility connectivity as the breakthrough point, each FTZ should build its network of multilevel connectivity in railroad, highway, aviation, shipping, communication, etc., in order to achieve connectivity with the countries along the B&R Initiative. (4) The FTZ can incubate local multinational corporations, which will lead to the radiation effect of the "B&R"

investment by applying their advantageous production capacity. (5) The four big FTZs should explore their own model of economic cooperation with the priority countries along the B&R Initiative. They might even consider to explore the space for in-depth cooperation between the enterprises of China and the priority countries along the B&R Initiative in the FTZ.

21.5 The Strategic Positioning of Each FTZ in the B&R Initiative

21.5.1 *The Strategic Positioning of Shanghai FTZ in the B&R Initiative*

In September 2013, Shanghai FTZ was officially established. It covers the total area reaching 120.72 km^2.

As the first domestic FTZ, Shanghai FTZ has accumulated certain experience in the system and mechanism innovation for the liberalization of investment and the facilitation of trade, etc., and possesses the advantage of a forerunner.

21.5.2 *The Strategic Positioning of Tianjin FTZ in the B&R Initiative*

Tianjin FTZ was officially established in April 2015. It covers a total area of 119.9 km^2.

The establishment of Tianjin FTZ was based on Tianjin Port, which is an important strategic fulcrum that connects the "Belt" and the "Road". Tianjin Port is the world's highest level of artificial deep-water port, North China's largest comprehensive port, the most convenient estuary port for the vast area of China's central and western regions, and the Central Asian countries. Tianjin Port is the only domestic port that possesses four lines of railroads which lead to the Eurasia Land Bridge, and is the nearest starting point in the east of the Eurasia Land Bridge. Financial leasing has become the highlight of the financial innovation of Tianjin, and could become the financing platform for the facility connectivity of the B&R Initiative.

21.5.3 *The Strategic Positioning of Fujian FTZ in the B&R Initiative*

In April 2015, Fujian FTZ was officially established. It covers a total area of 118.04 km².

Compared to Taiwan, Fujian possesses the advantage in land and labor resources. Fujian is both an important starting point of the MSR and the most important ancestral home for the overseas Chinese of Southeast Asia. The coastline of Fujian is the second longest in the country; Fujian FTZ contains excellent natural harbors.

Based on their distinct features, the three areas have different strategic positioning. Fuzhou area focuses on the manufacturing industry and the innovation of financing to achieve integrated currency flow; Pingtan area will focus on tourism industry, joint construction of the cross-Strait home land, promote the liberalization of investment and the facilitation of trade; Xiamen area will mainly focus on constructing the regional financial center, trade center, and demonstration zone for innovative industries and modern service industries across the strait.

Fujian is the important starting point of the MSR. Fujian enjoys a stable trade and economic relations with the Southeast Asian countries.

21.5.4 *The Strategic Positioning of Guangdong FTZ in the B&R Initiative*

Guangdong FTZ was officially established in April 2015. It covers an area of 116.2 km².

Shenzhen has always been a forefront of China's reform and opening-up. The city has a perfected market economy with outstanding open economy status, and has established an open-up pattern of omni-direction, multilevel and diverse industries. Qianhai is China's only pilot site for the innovative cross-border business of RMB.

Guangdong FTZ is to rely on Hong Kong and Macao, serve the domestic market, and face the world to explore a more open and more convenient rule of international investment and trade. Guangzhou Nansha New Area mainly focuses on developing the industries of shipping logistics, and international financing to achieve connectivity of facility and unimpeded flow of currencies. Shenzhen Qianhai Shekou Area mainly focuses on constructing the demonstration window of outward financial liberalization and forging the international hub port to achieve the facilitation of trade and the internationalization of financing. Zhuhai Hengqin New Area mainly focuses on developing the industries of tourism, leisure and health, business financial services, etc.

21.6 The Important Measures of the Differentiated Implementation of the B&R Initiative by Each FTZ

Each FTZ should capitalise on their advantages and strategic positioning to carry out the B&R Initiative in differentiation.

21.6.1 Shanghai FTZ Takes the Antecedence in Exploring the Rules and Mechanisms for the B&R Initiative Trade and Economic Cooperation

As the first domestic FTZ, Shanghai FTZ possesses the advantage of antecedence in the innovation of system and mechanism. It is the core force in constructing the new pattern of the open economy and forging version 2.0 openness of China. The system innovation of Shanghai FTZ mainly includes the following: investment management system with the negative list as the core; trade regulation system that focuses on trade facilitation, capital account convertibility and liberalized financial service; transformation of government function and the in-process and after-event supervision system.

> **Investment Management Model of Negative List.** Shanghai FTZ explores and implements the management model of the "pre-establishment national treatment + negative list" on foreign businesses; docks with the international high standards for the regulation system of investment and trade; lays foundation for China's participation in negotiation for bilateral and multilateral trade and economic cooperation and for protecting the interest of Chinese enterprises' "outgoing" investment.
> **Facilitation of Trade.** Build centers for commodity exhibition, sales, and procurement in countries and regions along the B&R Initiative.

The Internationalization of Financing. Extend the openness of financial service, etc. in FTZ, implement the capital account convertibility, achieve contra-flow in closed loop for the offshore RMB, create conditions for the B&R Initiative to achieve the important objectives and achieve the outgoing of both the production capacity and the currency.

The Maritime Connectivity. Based on the FTZ and the Yangshan deep-water port, establish the port and city alliances in the countries and regions along the MSR, and forge the Community of Common Destiny.

21.6.2 Construct the New, Open, Double-Way Platform and Channel of the B&R Initiative in Tianjin FTZ

Construct the New, Open, Double-Way Platform of the B&R. The establishment of Tianjin FTZ is based on Tianjin port. Tianjin port is an important port in foreign trade for Northeast, Northwest, and North China.

Build the New Pattern Trade Routes Based on the Continental Bridge Transportation of Tianjin Port. Optimize the network layout of ship routes to promote the construction of the maritime connectivity of the B&R Initiative; open up and increase the maritime ship routes that go through the continental bridge of Tianjin port to gradually perfect the global ship route network connected to Tianjin port. Explore the supply of goods in the market of the major regions in Japan, Korea, Central Asia, Mongolia, Russia, and Southeast Asia, construct the new channel of trade with Tianjin port as the transshipment port with the continental bridge as the link to connect Asia and Europe. Construct Tianjin port to became the important node port for the outbound tourists from China.

Construct the New Logistics Channels of the B&R Initiative. Construct the new logistics channels of the B&R Initiative through the construction of dry ports and logistics parks. Explore to build a dry port in Central Asia to extend the logistics network along the Silk Road Economic Belt; strengthen cooperation with Russia, Mongolia, and countries in Central Asia; plan for the construction of a logistics transit base in Tianjin port, and perfect the cross-border logistics service system.

Establish the Fulcrum for the Maritime Strategy. Tianjin FTZ possesses the advantage of concentration of industries; construction wise, it is comparatively a better port and adjacently located toward Japan and Korea.

Establish the Financial Leasing Market. The prioritized field in the construction of the B&R Initiative is the connectivity of facilities. The construction of infrastructure needs a large amount of capital input for the engineering machinery, which in turn increases the demand for the financial leasing industry.

21.6.3 Fujian FTZ Docks the Trade with Taiwan, Functionally Carries on the B&R Initiative

Fujian is both the FTZ and the core area of the MSR. It is the junction of the two strategies. The state's positioning for Fujian FTZ is to dock the trade with Taiwan, and functionally carry on the B&R Initiative.

Deepen the Docking with the Demonstration Zone of Taiwan FTZ. Trading with Taiwan is the most outstanding feature of Fujian FTZ. It should exert the advantage of the "five affinity", highlight the features of focusing on Taiwan. Fuzhou Area should focus on carrying on the transformation of Taiwan's high-tech industries to build the advanced manufacturing base. Xiamen Area should focus on the regional financial service center. Cross-Strait Pingtan Area should focus on the industries, such as tourism and cultural creativity, to became an international tourism island.

Construct the Cross-Straits Trade Center. Fujian FTZ should start with the "five connectivity", innovate the model of cooperation, reveal the strategic goal of MSR in terms of the function of the FTZ, promote the free flow of goods and services, promote further economic integration of Fujian and Taiwan, and promote the formation of the new, all-round, pattern of openness.

Construct the Cross-Strait Regional Financial Service Center. Fujian FTZ should innovate financial cooperation, establish the account and management model that adapts to the FTZ, set up the cross-Strait regional financial service center, promote the cross-border clearance business for RMB and the exchange business between RMB and NTD, establish the cross-Strait currency clearance center, achieve monetary circulation and create favorable conditions for the cross-Strait liberalization of investment and trade.

Construct the Cooperation Demonstration Zone of the Cross-Strait New Industries and Modern Service Industries. The objectives should be to promote in-depth openness toward Taiwan in the field of new industries and modern service industries, improve the free flow of personnel, capital, and service factors, and strengthen the cross-Strait cooperation in cross-Strait e-commerce, tourism, and medical services.

Construct the Southeast International Shipping Center. The Southeast international shipping center should serve as a carrier, improve the cooperation with the main ports (Taichung port, Hualien port, Kaohsiung port, Taipei port, etc.) and cities in Taiwan, promote maritime connectivity, and promote the joint construction of the MSR by both sides of the Strait. The joint construction of the MSR by both sides of the Strait will effectively expand the global influence raise the power of economy, produce more economic dividends, and will also be in line with the main stream of peaceful development of the cross-Strait relations and with the major direction of the cross-Strait cooperation.

Develop Marine Economy, Construct Maritime Strategic Fulcrum. Fujian is rich in marine resources. Fujian FTZ should focus on the marine economy, develop services related to offshore fishing industry, and expand the cooperation of marine economy with the countries along the MSR.

21.6.4 Functions of Guangdong FTZ

Focusing on Hong Kong and Macao, Guangdong FTZ will deepen the Guangdong-Hong Kong-Macao cooperation, construct the Guangdong-Hong Kong-Macao Big Bay Area, cooperate with major cities of the pearl river delta to jointly build the trade center that is to be the largest and the most powerful of its kind along the MSR.

Construct the Guangdong–Hong Kong–Macao Big Bay Area. Guangdong FTZ should expand the openness toward the Hong Kong and Macao region in the framework of Closer Economic Partnership Arrangement (CEPA) by eliminating invisible barriers, promoting further in-depth cooperation with Hong Kong and Macao, and building the Guangdong–Hong Kong–Macao Big Bay Area.

Build the Financial Hub and Investment Center of the Maritime Silk Road. Shenzhen Qianhai is the core area of Guangdong FTZ. It is also the most important base for the national financial opening and the "outgoing" of the RMB. Qianhai is to participate the construction of the 21st Century MSR and work with Hong Kong to become the financial hub and investment center of the MSR. In the construction course of the 21st Century MSR, the superiority of Hong Kong and Macao should be further exerted to become the platform for the economic cooperation between the hinterland and the countries along the MSR. "Shenzhen is a bridgehead, Qianhai is a strategic fulcrum, especially in terms of the modern service cooperation and through the strategic fulcrum of Qianhai. It can be extended to the countries and regions along the 21st Century Silk Road to promote the all-round cooperation."

Construct the International Logistics Hub Port of the Maritime Silk Road. There are two world-class groups of ports and airports near the FTZ with comparatively perfect infrastructure of ports and airports. Under the framework of the FTZ, Shekou port, Chiwan port, and Qianhai Bay port districts are linked together.

21.7 Functions of Fujian FTZ and Guangdong FTZ

Fujian FTZ will dock its trade with Taiwan, focus on the connectivity of the cross-Strait trade and policy, and construct the Fujian-Taiwan FTZ. Guangdong FTZ will focus on Hong Kong and Macao, emphasize on the connectivity of Guangdong, Hong Kong and Macao, and construct the Guangdong–Hong Kong–Macao Big Bay Area. Fujian, Guangdong, Hong Kong, Macao, and Taiwan should base on the Fujian–Taiwan FTZ and the Guangdong–Hong Kong–Macao Big Bay Area to jointly construct the "two shores, four places FTZ."

In addition, Fujian and Guangdong are both major ancestral homes for overseas Chinese. The overseas Chinese are a very important force in the construction of the FTZs, and are also an important bridge for the communication among the two shores and four places. They are also the participants and constructors of the MSR. They possess the advantage of promoting the "two shores, four places FTZ" and area constructing the MSR together.

Policy communication is the first priority in order to achieve discussion together, construction together and sharing together with the countries along the B&R Initiative. The overseas Chinese have a much superior role in connecting China and the foreign countries, and should become the bridge of policy communication.

CHAPTER 22

Status Quo of Port Cooperation Along the Maritime Silk Road

Li Ya

The Pacific Journal

22.1 Status Quo of Port Cooperation along the West Line of Maritime Silk Road

Maritime Silk Road (MSR), with its long history and rich spiritual significance, is endowed with a new mission in our new era. During his visit to the ASEAN countries in October 2013, President Xi Jinping, proposed for the first time that China will strengthen maritime cooperation with ASEAN countries by making good use of the China–ASEAN Maritime Cooperation Fund that is set up by the Chinese government and build the MSR of the 21st century by vigorously developing maritime partnership in a joint effort. In the implementation of the 21st Century MSR Initiative, President Xi further proposed the idea of "fostering regional cooperation from points (cities and ports) to surfaces and from lines to areas."

Ports, as important transport channels of the Belt and Road (B&R) Initiative and key hubs of the international transport system, are playing an increasingly significant role in international trade. The capacity, performance, and service provided by ports will affect the quality of goods transport, and transshipment. It affects the regional production system and the economy of a region. According to the "Vision and Actions on Jointly Building Silk Road Economic Belt and 21st Century MSR", that was jointly issued by the National Development and Reform Commission (NDRC), the Ministry of Foreign Affairs (MFA) and the Ministry of Commerce (MOFCOM) in March 2015, the 21st Century MSR has two lines: the western line and the southern line. For the purpose of in-depth analysis, this chapter focuses only on the western line, which stretches from the coast of China to the South China Sea, then to the Indian Ocean, and reaches Europe. The Initiative will focus on jointly building secured and efficient transport routes that connect the major sea ports along the B&R Initiative.

Although the MSR is in an early development stage and many countries along the road are taking a wait-and-see attitude, China has achieved substantial results (see Table 22.1) in port cooperation with countries along the road through approaches such as, overseas investment in port construction, investment in shares (holding), mergers and acquisitions and the signing of cooperation agreements between ports (mutually friendly port agreements and cooperation memorandums of understanding). The most remarkable achievements include cooperation with Port Klang of Malaysia, Port of Kyaukpyu of Myanmar, Port of Colombo of Sri Lanka, Gwadar Port of Pakistan, Port of Haifa of Israel, and Port of Piraeus of Greece, covering all major routes of the MSR, from which the following points can be concluded:

Cooperating closely with world-class ports along the MSR through mutual equity participation and port-to-port cooperation, as the core of the port cooperation network.

Cooperating with regional ports located along the MSR through investment in port construction, mergers, acquisitions and so on, as an important fulcrum of the port cooperation network.

Cooperating with oil ports and iron ore ports along the MSR through investment in shares, aid in port construction and so on, as an important complement to the port cooperation network.

A port cooperation network which is all-dimensional, multitiered and composite, as stated in the "Vision and Actions", is established.

Table 22.1: Major Achievements of China's Overseas Port Cooperation.

Region	Country	Port Project	Category of Cooperation
Southeast Asia	Myanmar	2015: Deep Water Port of Kyaukpyu invested by China went on trial operation 2015: The Port of Qingdao and the Port of Kyaiikpyu signed a friendly port agreement	Investment in Port Construction Port–port Corporation
	Vietnam	2010: China Merchants International invested in Vung Tau Container Terminal	Investment in non-controlling stakes
	Thailand	2015: Port of Guangzhou and Port of Laem Chabang signed a letter of intent on the conclusion of a friendly port agreement	Port–port Corporation
	Cambodia	2015: The Port of Qingdao and the Port of Sihanouk signed a friendly port agreement	Port–port Corporation
	Malaysia	2015: Beibu Bay Port in Guangxi Province and Port Klang concluded a friendly port agreement 2015: Port of Shenzhen and Port Klang concluded a friendly port agreement	Port–port Corporation Port–port Corporation
	Indonesia	2015: Port of Shenzhen and Indonesia Port Corporations concluded a friendly port agreement	Port–port Corporation

(*Continued*)

Table 22.1: (*Continued*)

Region	Country	Port Project	Category of Cooperation
South Asia	Sri Lanka	2014: China Harbor Engineering Co., Ltd. adopts the BOT model to build the port city of Colombo	Investment in port construction
		2011: China Merchants International Co., Ltd. invested in the construction and operation of the The Colombo South Container Terminal	Investment in port construction
		2008: China funded the construction of the Port of Hambantota	Investment in port construction
	Pakistan	2001 China invested in Gwadar port by invitation	Investment in port construction
		2013 China Overseas Port Holding Company, China Merchants International Co., Ltd. and China Ocean Shipping Group took over the right to operate Gwadar port	Investment in Controlling Stakes
		2015 Gwadar port became fully operational and was officially leased to China For 40 years	
	Bangladesh	2010: China funded the construction of the Port of Chittagong	Investment in port construction
The Middle East	Israel	2011; Port of Shanghai won the tender to operate Fort of Haifa for 25 years	Investment in non-controlling stakes
	Qatar	2011: China Harbor Engineering Co., Ltd. To build the first phase of the New Doha Port	Investment in port construction

(*Continued*)

Table 22.1: (*Continued*)

Region	Country	Port Project	Category of Cooperation
Europe	Greece	2009: China Ocean Shipping Group won the right to operate Piraeus 35 years	Investment in non-controlling stakes
	Belgium	2010: Shanghai International Port Group acquired 25% stake in the Port of Zeebrugge	Investment in non-controlling stakes
	France	1992–2015: Port of Shanghai signed friendly port agreements with Port Marseille, Le Havre and Dunkirk	Port–port Corporation
	The Netherlands	2005: The port of Shanghai and the port of Rotterdam concluded a friendly port agreement 2007: The port of Rotterdam became the first foreign friendly port of Shenzhen Port	Port–port Corporation

Source: News report and relevant literature.

Since the announcement of the 21st Century MSR, China's overseas port cooperation has developed several features: (1) Port development shifts from a unilateral approach to multilateral approach; (2) The rise of a more diversified combination of port cooperation. China's international port cooperation used to be predominantly port construction aid and equity participation, and recent years have witnessed the development model of investment in controlling stakes, BOT, and port enterprise contracting; (3) Cooperation shifts from being national interest-driven to regional interest-driven.

Countries and regions along the MSR are politically, economically, culturally, and geographically different, which requires different port cooperation strategies in order to promote port cooperation in a targeted approach. The following is a detailed analysis of the different areas involved in the construction of the Western Line.

Southeast Asia. Most countries in the region are island countries with economies mainly dependent on import and export. A port network has been established with the port of Singapore at its heart. The port cooperation between China and Southeast Asia is dominated by "port-to-port cooperation", which is mainly based on the Master Plan on China–ASEAN Port City Cooperation Network, promoting interport business through current port facilities and routes. The focuses of the cooperation are on port management, route design, resource sharing, information sharing, personnel training, and environmental protection, along with the construction of green, smart, and high-tech ports, in order to enhance bilateral trades and improve the service level.

South Asia. The region is located along the route of China's energy import, hence it is crucial to the security of China's maritime energy transport channel. South Asian ports are not only of great strategic significance to China, but some are also the important fulcrum of China's western region opening to the outside world, connecting China with the Middle East and Africa.

The Middle East. The Middle East is China's main source of oil import. It is also an important area of major power games, so the investment and cooperation environment is rather complicated. The majority of ports in the Middle East are built for oil export, so most of them are oil terminals; recent years, nonetheless, have witnessed the development of specialized terminals, such as container and bulk terminals. The focus of China–Middle East port cooperation should be the joint operation of ports, the goals being a global strategic layout of port and shipping enterprises and China's energy import security.

Europe. The European ports have a long history and many of them are modernized international ports with solid infrastructure and advanced management. However, the major European ports have been declining remarkably since the European debt crisis. The focus of China–Europe port cooperation should be investment and equity participation, and areas of cooperation include port investment, terminal operation, and logistics industry. The port network in this region can bring down the trade cost between the two sides and facilitate the maritime channel of China's import and export.

22.2 Status Quo of Port Cooperation along the Maritime Silk Road in Southeast Asia and Port Cooperation within ASEAN Countries

Southeast Asia is where the western and southern routes of the 21st Century MSR overlap and it is the starting point of the construction of the MSR.

ASEAN countries are all maritime nations except Laos. Maritime interconnectivity has been an important ASEAN strategy in the past two decades. Container throughput is considered an important indicator of port development. The container throughput of ASEAN countries increased from 400,000 TEU to 88 million TEUs from 1975 to 2013. ASEAN accounted for 2.3% of the world's container throughput in 1975, and that number rose to 13.5% in 2013. Singapore's container throughput was 33.5 million TEUs in 2013, accounting for 38.1% of ASEAN countries, while Malaysia and Indonesia accounted for 24.3% and 12.2%, respectively. The three countries ranked the second, the fifth, and the ninth in the world, respectively, and the total amount of container throughput of the three countries accounted for 80% of the ASEAN total. However, the quality of port facilities in ASEAN countries, except Singapore, needs to be improved.

Since the Asian financial crisis in 1997, ASEAN has been committed to building a platform for port cooperation to enhance regional trade and integration. In 1999, the ASEAN Framework Agreement on Transport Cooperation proposed the establishment of the "ASEAN Port System", in which 33 ports were included. In 2000, the number of the ports increased to 46. Since 2007, ASEAN has unified the port standard and integrated the ASEAN shipping market and the ASEAN port network into the ASEAN logistics network. In May 2011, ASEAN released the Master Plan on ASEAN Interconnectivity to strengthen interconnectivity for the first time, and put maritime interconnectivity at the heart of ASEAN interconnectivity.

22.3 China–ASEAN Port Cooperation

China is currently the largest trading partner of ASEAN, and ASEAN is China's third largest trading partner. The two parties have built the world's largest free trade area of developing countries, and cooperation between the two in maritime interconnectivity is accelerating.

First, from the perspective of China–ASEAN maritime cooperation, 13 meetings have been held since the first China–ASEAN Ministerial Conference on Transport in 2002. The two sides established the China–ASEAN Transport Consultation Mechanism in 2003. In 2010, China and ASEAN signed the Memorandum of Understanding on Maritime Consultation Mechanism, which aims at strengthening the cooperation in port management, maritime traffic safety, navigation assistance, and crew training and certification. China and ASEAN have established the China–ASEAN Maritime Cooperation Partnership and formulated the Master Plan on China–ASEAN Connectivity. China announced the establishment of the China–ASEAN Maritime Cooperation Fund in 2011 and the China–ASEAN port city cooperation network, which was among the first 17 shortlisted projects of the Fund.

Second, China has established maritime cooperation mechanism with some ASEAN member countries. In 2010, for example, China and Indonesia signed the Minutes of the Meeting on Strengthening Trade and Investment Cooperation between China and Indonesia. In 2012, China and Malaysia signed an agreement on maritime transport. In addition, China is working with Singapore to build Dalian container terminal, and China has also invested in the construction of Kyaukpyu port in Myanmar.

Third, with the establishment of the Beibu Gulf Economic Rim and the construction of the MSR, the Pan-Beibu Gulf area has become the regional logistics base, trade base and processing base of China and ASEAN. Provincial regions such as Guangxi, Guangdong, and Fujian established maritime partnership with ASEAN. Fangcheng, Fuzhou, Qinzhou, Guangzhou, and other ports have become key cities along the 21st Century MSR, as well as transport hubs connecting China and ASEAN.

The China–ASEAN port city cooperation network, which was established in 2013, is a flagship project to promoting maritime interconnectivity.

The project is committed to implementing the consensus between China and ASEAN leaders on "building a maritime interconnectivity network" and "developing pragmatic maritime cooperation", focusing on promoting the comprehensive cooperation between China–ASEAN port cities in areas such as mutual navigation, port construction, port industry, maritime exchanges, and cultural tourism. The project will facilitate the construction of shipping logistics circle, port cooperation circle, industry park cooperation circle, tourism cooperation circle, and friendly city cooperation circle among port cities.

The first seven projects of the China–ASEAN port city cooperation network are going smoothly, with some of the projects having been put into service in China–ASEAN port transportation. The first phase of China–ASEAN Port Logistics Information Center has been completed. The China–ASEAN port, route, and shipping services have been in place.

With the upgraded version of the China–ASEAN Free Trade Agreement (FTA), the growth of bilateral trade will bring higher requirement for port cooperation and logistics network construction. Meanwhile, with the zero-tariff policy and the opening up of the ASEAN markets and investment, the two sides are in an advantageous position to strengthen the port cooperation network.

22.4 Thoughts and Suggestions on Port Cooperation along the Maritime Silk Road

The B&R Initiative is brought up against the backdrop of the international power structure transition from quantitative to qualitative changes, the short-term setback of economic globalization, the increase of geopolitical and geoeconomic issues, the Asia–Pacific re-adjustment, and the profound identity shift of China as a major power. Here are some thoughts and suggestions.

First, the understanding of Islamic civilization, maritime civilization, and underdeveloped areas in Eurasia by China lags behind that of Christian civilization and the developed western world. The B&R Initiative provides a historical opportunity for China and countries along it economically, politically, and culturally. This would profoundly change the geopolitical and geoeconomic landscape in Eurasia and the relations between the Pacific and the Atlantic, which may need realignment.

Second, with the advancement of the construction of the 21st Century MSR, we should understand "land–sea coordination" from a realistic perspective. It is put forward in the first place that we modify the long-held prejudice against maritime development of China, as China had been of agricultural culture for long and later this idea embodied the revaluation on the balance between land power and sea power. The countries along the MSR have different locations and development paths. Take Pakistan and Sri Lanka, for example. Pakistan has the China–Pakistan Economic Corridor as land support and the Gwadar port project enjoys greater inland capacity and support — in other words, a larger space for sea-to-land development. Sri Lanka, in comparison, is more sea-oriented. Besides, there are more opportunities along the land Silk Road than the MSR. The construction of the B&R Initiative should consider land development as a priority over sea development. In summary, when building the MSR, the "land-sea coordination" entails more realistic planning and arrangements under different circumstances.

Finally, Southeast Asia is the pilot area and gateway of the "21st Century MSR", the China–ASEAN maritime interconnectivity serves as an important model. The South China Sea disputes are unlikely to be resolved in the short term. The strategy package will stabilize the region, preventing some countries inside and outside the region to undermine regional cooperation. Pan-Beibu Gulf area is the frontier of China–ASEAN interconnectivity. However, there are some problems in the region: homogeneous competition among the ports exist in this area, and coordination is absent in the port development; some logistics enterprises around these ports are lagging behind in information technology. By taking advantage of ports and inland support to improve regional industrial chains, the Pan-Beibu Gulf would serve as a solid foundation for deepening the interconnectivity with ASEAN countries.

CHAPTER 23

The Belt and Road Initiative and Production Capacity Cooperation between China and India

Chen Lijun

*Institute of South Asia Studies, Yunnan Academy
of Social Sciences, Kumming, China*

23.1 Introduction

International production capacity cooperation is a mutually beneficial cooperation among countries in construction, trade, investment, expansion, upgrading, transfer and application of production capacity. Promoting China's competitive production capacity to "go global" and promoting international production capacity cooperation will contribute to the optimization and transformation of China's industrial structure, enhance international competitiveness of Chinese companies, expand development space, and realize complementary advantages, mutual benefits, and common development with related countries. India, as a big power of South Asia that is adjacent to China, has rapidly developed its economy in recent years and is actively implementing the "Made in India" strategy in order to attract foreign investment and promote economic development. These are all favorable conditions for both sides to strengthen the production capacity cooperation. China should seize the favorable opportunity and take measures actively to promote the production capacity cooperation with India so as to achieve mutual benefit and common development.

23.2 Significance of Strengthening Production Capacity Cooperation between China and India

International production capacity cooperation and international industrial transfer are closely linked; also, industrial transfer and international investment are closely linked. As economic development strategies, economic development levels, and industrial structures are different from country to country, international production capacity cooperation and industrial transfer happen frequently. As for the reasons why the international production capacity cooperation happens, scholars from various countries have conducted extensive researches. Among them, the most famous theories are the Product Life Cycle, the Marginal Industry Expansion, and the Eclectic Paradigm of International Production brought up by Raymond Vernon in Harvard University, Kiyoshi Kojima in Hitotsubashi University, and John H. Dunning in University of Reading, respectively.

As neighboring countries, China and India are both rising. However, the mutual investment is relatively small and the production capacity cooperation is limited. From the perspective of trade, since the 21 Century, bilateral trade between China and India has maintained a steady growth. The trade volume has increased rapidly from US$ 2.9 billion in 2000 to US$ 71.62 billion in 2015, a 23-fold increase during 15 years. China and India have become the largest trading partners in South Asia. Meanwhile, China–India trade development is increasingly uneven, India's trade deficit to China was US$ 10 billion at the beginning of this century, and it reached US$ 44.857 billion in 2015. Under the context of the construction of the B&R Initiative, strengthening production capacity cooperation between China and India would be significant for each other's economic development, as discussed in this section.

23.2.1 *Jointly Deal with Challenges of Economic Globalization and Easing the Pressure of Economic Downturn*

In recent years, with the globalization of the world economy and the integration of regional economy, the global trade and investment liberalization has been further developed; various types of free trade zones are emerging, and the world economic interdependence is greatly increased. In the context of accelerating globalization of the world economy and slow recovery of the current world economy, China and India should strengthen their production capacity cooperation, which will be beneficial to the joint efforts in coping with the challenges of globalization.

23.2.2 *Joint Promotion of Development, Transformation, and Upgrading of Industries*

After years of development, China's economic power has strengthened significantly. China has not only stepped into the latter stage of industrialization, but also greatly raised its financial strength. Under the "new normal" status of the economy, China needs to change the traditional mode of economic development, strengthen the impetus conversion, adjust the stock, optimize the increment, and promote the economic structure from the low end to high end. The industrial development status of China and India reveals a tremendous opportunity for production capacity cooperation.

23.2.3 *Improve Trade Balance and Deepen Economic Integration*

The trade imbalance after the expansion of trade scale has increasingly become an obstacle in expanding economic and trade cooperation between China and India, so they need to strengthen production capacity cooperation.

There are many reasons for the trade imbalance between China and India. One important reason is that the levels of industrial development of both sides are not the same. In 2014, India's main exports to China included cotton, copper, copper products, minerals, organic chemicals, and fossil fuels. Among them, cotton valued US$ 2.80 billion, copper and copper products valued US$ 2.10 billion, and fossil fuel valued US$ 1.5 billion, accounting for 21.0%, 15.5%, and 11.3% of India's total exports to China, respectively, and accounting for 47.8% in total. India's imports of goods from China were mainly mechanical and electrical products, machinery and equipment, organic chemicals, fertilizers, steel, plastic products. These six categories of goods amounted to US$ 38.7 billion, accounting for 66.4% of India's total imports from China. These made China's trade surplus with India grow. In June 2015, China–India Forum on Economic, Trade and Tourism Cooperation was held in Kunming. Indian Minister of State for External Affairs V.K. Singh said that the trade imbalance between India and China was not in the long-term interests for both India and China.

Production capacity cooperation is helpful for the two sides to achieve mutual benefit and win–win situation. The economic integration is to open up to each other, break the barriers that constrain regional economic development, give full play to their comparative advantages, nurture the main industrial sectors and pillars, and promote economic integration and regional economic development.

23.2.4 *Improve Sino-Indian Relations*

There are many aspects in promoting bilateral relations between China and India, among which economic relations is the most important one. India has long faced current account and budget deficits. According to the Chinese Consulate General in Mumbai, India, the budget deficit of fiscal year 2016–2017 may account for 3.7% or 3.9% of India's GDP. The first reason is that India has been implementing a separate finance system between the central and the local governments. The central government's tax revenue is limited. Second, it can help to expand the economic scale and promote economic development. India, as "world office", has relative advantages in the IT, services, and pharmaceutical industries. Third, it can cultivate new industries and enhance economic competitiveness. India is developing various types of industrial parks, building "industrial economic corridor", and appropriated 70.6 billion rupees as special funds to build 100 "smart cities" nationwide. Fourth, it can cultivate talents for the better development of industries. India is promoting the "Made in India" strategy, expecting that the proportion of manufacturing sector in economy will rise up to 25% in 2022 from the current 16%. India announced the Foreign Trade Policy 2015–2020 (FTP) which aims at promoting manufacturing development, services exports, employment growth, also reducing corporate taxes, tariffs, liberalizing the restrictions of foreign direct Investment, and stimulating domestic investment. Fifth, it can improve infrastructure construction. The lagging infrastructure has become a serious impediment to India's development. On 28 February, 2015, Indian Finance Minister Arun Jaitley published for the first time India's fiscal budget since Prime Minister Modi took office and announced that the government would spend US$ 11.3 billion on infrastructure projects, such as roads, railways, ports, and sanitation. Promoting production capacity cooperation not only optimizes the allocation of resources and achieves mutual benefit and common development, but also helps to eliminate the distrust between the two countries.

23.2.5 *Promote Complementary Advantages, Mutual Benefit and Win–Win Situation*

Mutual benefit and common development are the basis for building a new strategic partnership between China and India. Although China's economy has not yet entered the Lewis turning point, the industrialization and urbanization are not yet over, the benefits of reform and opening-up policy continue to be realized. Generally speaking, it has entered the "new normal" stage. Although India's manufacturing industry is relatively underdeveloped, there is labor resource that is relatively cheap and has a vast market.

23.3 Status of China's Foreign Direct Investment and China–India Production Capacity Cooperation

23.3.1 *Status of China's Foreign Direct Investment*

According to the Statistical Bulletin of China's Foreign Direct Investment published by the Ministry of Commerce, the National Bureau of Statistics and the State Administration of Foreign Exchange, in 1990, China's net foreign investment (also known as flow) was only US$ 900 million. In 2014, foreign investment reached US$ 123.12 billion, which increased by 14.2% over the previous year, China became the world's third largest foreign investment country. In the late 1990s, China's stock of foreign direct investment was over US$ 20 billion, rising to US$ 57.2 billion in 2005 and US$ 882.64 billion in 2014, accounting for 3.4% of global outflow stock of foreign direct investment from 0.4% in 2002, ranking eighth in the world. In the B&R Initiative national investment, investment toward transportation, electricity, telecommunications and other competitive industries values about US$ 11.66 billion. By the end of 2015, China's stock of foreign direct investment had exceeded trillion dollars. By December 2015, there had been 75 cooperation areas under the promotion of Chinese enterprises. 2015 was called "the first year" of China's international production capacity cooperation, for China took a new step to promoting international production capacity cooperation in the year.

23.3.2 *Status of China–India Production Capacity Cooperation*

According to the statistics from the Chinese Customs, the bilateral trade volumes between China and India were US$ 2.9 billion and 7 billion, respectively, in 2000 and 2004, and the volume reached US$ 38 billion in 2008, and it was up to US$ 65.471 billion in 2013. According to India's Ministry of Commerce Information and Statistics and Ministry of Commerce and Industry, China–India bilateral trade in 2013 amounted to US$ 65.95 billion (of which India's export to China was US$ 14.56 billion, and import from China was US$ 51.39 billion), India's trade deficit with China was US$ 36.83 billion. India's "Financial Express" website reported on 2 March, 2014 that China has become the top trading partner with India, followed by the United States and the United Arab Emirates. China–India trade reached US$ 71.62 billion in 2015, which increased by 1.4% over the previous year. China's export to India was US$ 58.24 billion, which increased by 7.4%; China's import from India was US$ 13.383 billion, down by 18.35%. China's trade surplus with India was US$ 44.857 billion, with a growth of 18.52%.

By the end of 2014, China's engineering contract in India totaled US$ 64 billion; the completed cumulative revenue reached US$ 41.3 billion. So far, there are more than 500 Chinese enterprises in India having operational projects.

The cooperation between the two countries in the fields of electric power, transportation, information, and medicine has developed well. After the establishment of the joint ventures, the expected annual sales may amount to 10 billion yuan or more. One of the most important joint ventures is the anti-tumor and anti-AIDS drug production in Henan Province, China. In addition, there are 10 Indian banks that have set up four branches and nine representative offices in China with total assets of 2.75 billion yuan.

23.4 India's Plan to Strengthen Production Capacity Cooperation with China

In August 2014, Prime Minister of India, Narendra Modi announced a "Make in India" plan to forge India into a world-class manufacturing center and launched it in September. The goal of the proposal is to increase the share of manufacturing in the economy from the current 15% to 25%, and to create 12 million jobs each year, as well as to develop India into a major globalized country of manufacturing and exporting.

After the B&R initiative, China proposed and established the Asian Infrastructure Investment Bank (AIIB) and the Silk Road Fund. India has become a significant member of the AIIB and the BRIC Development Bank. In July 2014, Prime Minister Modi met with President Xi Jinping during his attendance in the sixth BRIC summit in Brazil, he expressed his embracement of more Chinese investment to India. China has decided to invest US$ 20 billion in India's industry and infrastructure sectors over the next five years. There are very good opportunities for cooperation in infrastructure construction, tourism, manufacturing, and other fields for two countries, they should jointly grasp the market opportunities. The two sides agreed to carry out some feasibility study, including speeding-up of India Chennai–Bangalore–Mysore section and high-speed railway between Delhi and Nagpur. Prime Minister Modi said at the "China–India Economic and Trade Forum" that India has further adjusted the policies and improved the environment so that Chinese enterprises can carry out business activities in India in a "convenient and comfortable" manner. In June 2015, Indian Foreign Minister of State for External Affairs V.K. Singh said that the prospect of cooperation between China and India is bright. He hoped that the two sides would deeply promote exchanges and cooperation in infrastructure, railways, economic corridors, and smart cities.

23.5 Countermeasures and Suggestions to Accelerate China–India Production Capacity Cooperation

23.5.1 *Establishing Production Capacity Cooperation Mechanism and Production Capacity Cooperation Fund*

China and India can actively promote the establishment of investment summit or hold the China–India Investment Summit during China–South Asia Expo to promote the effective docking of industrial policies and investment policies, thereby expanding production capacity cooperation. China has established production capacity cooperation funds with Kazakhstan, Latin America, and Africa.

23.5.2 *Facilitation of Trade and Investment*

The most important thing is to break the barriers in traffic, trade, and investment, to promote facilitation of trade and investment and to improve the investment environment substantially. First, promote facilitation by establishing FTA. Second, accelerate the construction of connectivity. Third, improve the investment environment. Public and private joint ventures and private projects must obtain agreement from 70% to 80% of the land owners in advance. An example is the labor policy. India's Labor Act provides that enterprises with more than 100 employees must be approved by government when it needs to lay-off workers. Fourth, strengthen communication and coordination of interests, speed up the free flow of elements of production, and create a fair and open environment for cooperation.

23.5.3 *Priority Areas of Cooperation*

Strengthening production capacity cooperation between China and India can not only promote the strategy docking between "Made in China 2025" and "Make in India", but can also achieve complementary advantages and common development.

23.5.4 *Deepening Financial Cooperation*

Production capacity cooperation requires financial support. First, set up more financial branches mutually to accelerate the direct settlement between rupee and renminbi. Second, expand the scale of currency swap. Third, promote the mutual opening up in financial industry and accelerate the free flow of financial elements. Fourth, put forward exchanges and cooperation between central banks and financial institutions of the two sides. Fifth, build the information flow platform. Sixth, promote production capacity cooperation by making full use of BRIC National Bank, AIIB, and Silk Road Fund.

23.6 Improving the Level of Mutual Political Trust

Mutual trust is the basis for expanding capacity cooperation. China and India hold far more common interests than differences. The two sides should focus on the overall situation, tolerating and referencing each other mutually, shelving disputes, controlling differences, and strengthening the protection of the interests of investment enterprises.

23.7 Deepening Mutual Understanding

China and India are not only quite different in their systems, economic development models, business environments, religious beliefs, customs, and habits, but every province in India also varies widely in development policies and levels. All these reasons lead to the different investment environments, market opportunities, and development prospects.

23.8 Actively Facing Investment Risks

There are many kinds of risks, including politics, economy, law, social culture, and natural disasters. Different risks need to be coped with in different ways, but the most important thing is that everyone does a good job at his own post. First, the two countries should adhere to mutual benefit and common development. Second, they must pay attention to joint venture operations. Third, they must abide by laws and regulations. Fourth, India and China should actively negotiate and resolve various contradictions and disputes. Fifth, there should be enhanced awareness of safety measures. Sixth, an emergency response mechanism should be developed.

CHAPTER 24

Suggestions on Promoting the Coordinated Development of the Belt and Road Construction and Western Development

Quan Yi

China National Committee for Pacific Economic Cooperation
(PECC-China) and DPP Central Liaison Committee,
China–ASEAN Institute of Guangxi University, Guangxi, China

24.1 Introduction

China's Western Development marks the transition from a gradient development strategy to a balanced development strategy. However, only limited achievements have been made since the implementation of the strategy in 1999 and the development gap between the eastern and western China has been widening. In 2013, President Xi Jinping raised the initiative of jointly building the Silk Road Economic Belt (SREB) and the 21 Century Maritime Silk Road (MSR) during his visit in central Asian country Kazakhstan and ASEAN country Indonesia, which was a major adjustment to China's opening-up policy and layout of the geopolitical economy. The central government has placed the western region as the front platform to implement the Westward Strategy and develop the Belt and Road (B&R) Initiative. Chinese enterprises are provided with a historic opportunity in Western Development when they transfer to the Silk Road via the western region.

However, if these Chinese enterprises only took the western region as a passageway when they moved to the Silk Road, West China would collapse and become the vulnerable part of the world economic development and remain in poverty. This strategy has achieved little due to China's high logistic price. The logistic costs of shipping raw materials from overseas to Guangdong, then to Hunan, Jiangxi or Guangxi, and then exporting the products are way too high to cover labor, land and other costs. Therefore, most Chinese enterprises choose to invest directly in Southeast Asia and Africa rather than invest in Central and West China. Here, both the poor investment environment and the distance from the market in the central and western regions, and factors such as China's inefficient policies of regional development account for the results.

Since 2000, China has implemented at least seven regional economic policies, including Western China Development, Northeast China Revitalization Plan, and Rise of Central China Plan — the three of the highest standard with the documents issued by the CPC Central Committee and the State Council at the same time and coordinated by national institutes. The "eastern region taking the lead in development" policy is also one of the seven policies. The other three main plans, following the 18th National Congress of the CPC, are the B&R Initiative, coordinated development of the Beijing, Tianjin, and Hebei region, and Yangtze River Economic Belt. All these three regional plans have set up national coordinating bodies with Zhang Gaoli, member of the Standing Committee of the Political Bureau of the CPC Central Committee and Vice Premier of China as the head of the leading group. There are many other provincial development plans that have risen to national strategies. In fact, the central government gives the most preferential policies to Shanghai, Zhejiang, Fujian, and Guangdong, the richest places in China, while the poorest places like Tibet, Shaanxi, Gansu, and Qinghai receive fewer national preferential policies. This is the root of the solidification and the continued expansion of the regional development gap in China.

24.2 Coordinated Development of Western Development and Silk Road

To construct the B&R Initiative, one important issue that must be solved is how to make the best of the western region and promote its development and opening-up.

First, speeding up the development of the western region is necessary not only for a balanced development of China and narrowing the regional gap, but also for expanding the domestic market to achieve sustained economic development. The Western Development strategy should be given strategic priority in China's opening toward the west. If the vast western border region merely serves as a channel, the western region would not get any practical benefit or development in the Silk Road construction. Therefore, the implementation of the Western Development strategy should take precedence over the construction of the SREB. Shifting the Eastern and domestic resources in investment to the western region is an important approach to the expansion of China's domestic demand as well as keeping the roots and avoiding industrial hollowing out.

Second, the formation of the national unified market and the system of regional economic fragmentation is an important prerequisite for regional coordinated development. The eastern and western domestic economic integration and national integration are of particular significance for eliminating geographical and ethnic differences and maintaining the border security and long-term stability. Eliminating the disparity of regional development and the gap between the east and the west is the key to national integration. Hence, in realizing the connectivity and aligning the industrial capacity of China and countries along the B&R Initiative, priority should be given to the establishment of the regional fragmentation and a unified domestic market through the coordination between the development of China's border areas and the eastern region.

Third, the central government should plan the B&R Initiative and the Western Development Strategy as a whole, giving priority to the connectivity between China and neighboring countries. The Silk Road construction is based on "five connectivity". Facilities connectivity is the foundation while capacity cooperation and cultural exchanges are the support. Hence, the infrastructure construction and development planning in western China should be linked to the construction and development of the Silk Road. When coordinating the industrial capacity and development in the construction of the Eurasian Continental Bridge, the China–Pakistan Economic Corridor, the China–ASEAN Interconnection, the Sino-Mongolian–Russia Economic Corridor, the connectivity of China and Central Asia, etc., the government should also include Central and Western China. Among all the regions, the construction of channels connecting China and other countries via Guangxi, Yunnan, Tibet, Xinjiang, Inner Mongolia, Heilongjiang and other border areas needs overall planning.

China–Myanmar oil and gas pipelines have been built in the construction of the Bangladesh–China–India–Myanmar Economic Corridor, but the railways and highways have not yet been connected. The construction of Burma Road during the War of Resistance against Japanese Aggression War (Stilwell Road) shows that it is of great strategic significance, especially for the development and opening up of the Southwestern China.

At present, China has obtained the right to operate the Gwadar port. China's oil shipping will no longer need to take the 12,000 km route passing Malacca Strait but directly take the pipelines or high-speed rails from Gwadar port, which only covers about 2,400 km to enter Kashgar. But the construction of the China–Pakistan Economic Corridor must be closely coordinated with the development and construction of southern Xinjiang, such as Kashgar, as it is a major strategic issue related to the security of the western region.

Oil and gas pipelines of China–Russia and Central Asia have been built, but railways and highways need to be upgraded. The Great Eurasian Economic Partnership proposed by the Russian President Putin aligns the Russia-led Eurasian Federation and the Shanghai Cooperation Organization. In this case, China can put the establishment of the China–Eurasian Free Trade Zone on the agenda after which China's north-line energy supply and market stability will be secured. Therefore, the construction of the SREB should be connected with the Western Development, making the western region a bridge linking the Eurasian continent.

Fourth, western China should play its role of an important bridge connecting China and the surrounding areas. Following the opening-up policy and facilities connectivity, the border's role will shift from the shielding effect into the intermediary effect and become a bridge connecting China and other countries. Enterprises of eastern China will need to establish a front base in the western region, while the western region will provide intermediary services for eastern enterprises to enter the SREB. China's western region is the transition zone between China and Central Asia, featuring a great language and cultural diversity: a majority of China's minority groups of Kazak, Uyghur, Hui are living in this area, bearing an inextricably link with the Central Asian culture. Also, many ethnic groups in Yunnan have strong ties of blood, culture, and business with ethnic groups in Myanmar. When entering a strange country, enterprises from eastern China can take advantage of these human resources and cultural resources.

Fifth, the opening up and security issues of the border should be considered as a whole. Due to the division of government departments in China, the implementation of the opening-up policy is faced with mutual constraints. Border control authorities and commodity inspection departments show a huge difference in terms of both attitudes and acts when giving permissions to vehicles from the surrounding countries to enter China. The current failure of vehicles' attempt to enter China from Central Asian and Southeast Asian countries is related to security issues, which has caused doubts in peripheral countries about the connectivity that China advocates as they fear that their own security could face threats. For example, India is full of worries over the construction of the China–Pakistan Economic Corridor, so is Myanmar over the Yunnan–Burma railway construction. Due to the lack of mutual trust in policies, there are difficulties in customs clearance for either personnel or vehicles. The protection barriers set up for each other have also added to the difficulty of initiating investment projects and have caused many cooperative projects to end in vain. It is a challenge for China to figure out approaches to eliminate the security worries of neighboring countries and increase mutual trust in policies. The LAM provides a solution that is to build a comprehensive cooperation mechanism which covers economic development, social and cultural exchanges, and political security.

24.3 Need for New Policies and New Initiatives in Western Development

China's coordinated development of the eastern and western regions is mainly through partner assistance, arranging the developed eastern regions to support their twinning partners in the backward western areas. The government should play its role of orientation and guide both domestic and foreign markets (enterprises) to participate in the development of the western region. The Western Development Strategy needs new policies and new initiatives.

First, the differentiated strategy of regional development should be carried out to guide the eastern enterprises to move westward and promote the rapid development of the western region. China's regional development policies should have strategic planning instead of rent-seeking of local governments. Regional development strategies should have a clear objective to reduce the gap between the rich and the poor among regions. China should strengthen the top-level design for the development of backward areas in the west, giving them more support in preferential policies, equalization of public services, industrial development planning, human resources development, opening-up, and development of international trade. Regional development planning and policies of the central government must reflect regional differences corresponding to the sustainable development of national regions and national strategies of poverty alleviation and poverty reduction. The industrial development should reflect the differentiated fiscal and taxation policies. For enterprises investing in the western region, preference should be given in the land acquisition (providing cheap land for industrial parks), tax concessions (tax-relief for five years or income tax levied at 15%), and relocation cost subsidy. Special human resources development policies should also be implemented, such as giving those enterprises that organize off-site training and increase employment incentives both tax relief and direct subsidies in finance and taxation. But in carrying out the preferential policies, resources must be channeled and equalitarianism must be avoided.

Second, the planning of the Silk Road industrial capacity cooperation should be aligned with the planning of the western industrial development. The amount of resources in China differs greatly from region to region. To promote the transfer of industries from the eastern region to the central and western regions, fresh ideas are needed: apart from transferring the eastern manufacturing and trade enterprises to the west, the government should encourage the industries to shift from importing raw materials from overseas to exploiting the low-cost local resources for production. Also, the focus of the sales should shift back from overseas markets to the domestic eastern market or to countries along the Silk Road via western China. In fact, many industries in coastal areas have their raw materials sent from the western region. The husbandry in the west provides skin and wool which along with raw materials like cotton from Xinjiang are supplied the eastern enterprises. Hence, the transportation costs were increased. If industries of this kind in the east were transferred to the western region, the formation of regional fragmentation system and a national unified market should have better prospects for development.

Third, the industrial transfer should be combined with the Western Development and poverty alleviation strategies. The keys are targeted poverty alleviation, improvement of the production and living conditions of residents in the western region, equalization of public services, infrastructure improvement, and industrial poverty alleviation. The living environment in many parts of the western region is rather poor. For these areas, farmers and herdsmen need to be relocated. To make these residents willing to move out, live a stable life, and get out of poverty afterward, industry poverty alleviation is the key. Marketing also needs to be strengthened.

Fourth, the central government should introduce more policies to develop the border area and improve people's income, and at the same time innovate new border cooperation modes. Here are some suggestions: expand the pace of opening up along the border areas and set up free trade zones and cross-border economic cooperation zones in important cities along border areas; implement special methods and policies at key borders, and in border cities and economic cooperation zones to promote personnel exchanges, logistics and tourism; support the inland cities to open airports, dry ports, or free ports and eventually form an opened economic corridor; establish financial institutions focusing on development to accelerate infrastructural connections among neighboring countries and regions.

Fifth, it is proposed that the western strategic production projects formed during the Third Front Movement be revitalized. In modern times, the national defense power system was shifted to mechanical force. In 1873, Zuo Zongtang set up the Lanzhou Manufacturing Bureau, which laid the material foundation for the subsequent smashing of the Yaquber Rebellion and the stabilization of Xinjiang. In 1860, Zuo Zongtang set up the Lanzhou Machine Weaving Bureau. After the founding of People's Republic of China, for the realization of the strategic depth and the establishment of the strategic rear, Lanzhou, Chongqing, Chengdu, Guizhou Anshun, Golmud, and Karamay were listed as key cities in the strategic layout in the First Five-Year Plan and the Third Front Movement. Thirty out of the 156 key projects that laid the foundation of China's new industry were located in Lanzhou, Qinghai Atomic City, Golmud, Chengdu, and Kunming. Today, while focusing on creating eco-friendly cities in the western region, we must not neglect the strategic security function of these Third Front Movement bases in maintaining the security and stability of the whole rear area.

Sixth, it is suggested that Kashi Special Economic Zone be built as the key node in the China–Pakistan Economic Corridor and the security barrier of West China. Kashi is the key city in southern China, the security barrier of the western regions of China, the joint point of the SREB and the MSR, and the center of China–Pakistan Economic Corridor. With the promotion of SREB Initiative and the construction of the China–Pakistan Economic Corridor, Kashi Special Economic Zone will become the hub of communication between China and Western Asia, and Kashi's strategic position will continue to strengthen. Historically, Kashi is the west end of China westward development with its importance to the security of the country being a consistent focus of the central government in different eras. From the first opening of the western channel by Ban Chao in Han Dynasty, Gao Xianzhi in Tang Dynasty, Zuo Zongtang in Qing Dynasty, Kashi has been always given the highest border military.

Index

CPSIA information can be obtained
at www.ICGtesting.com
Printed in the USA
BVHW040500140519
548193BV00004BA/8/P